EARTHRISE

ALSO BY JEFF APPELQUIST

NONFICTION

Changing Places: Travels in a Vanishing World

Legacy of Excellence: A Centennial History of the Toro Company

Wisdom Is Not Enough: Reflections on Leadership & Teams

*Sacred Ground: Leadership Lessons from
Gettysburg & the Little Bighorn*

FICTION

The Great Wild West: An American Journey

EARTH

Leadership Lessons from the Apollo Space Missions

RISE

JEFF APPELQUIST

AWARD-WINNING AUTHOR OF
SACRED GROUND

ISBN-13: 978-1-63489-550-7

Cover and interior design by Emily Rodvold.

Printed in the United States of America
First Printing: 2022

26 25 24 23 22   5 4 3 2 1

Wise Ink Creative Publishing
807 Broadway St. NE, Suite 46
Minneapolis, MN 55413
www.wiseink.com

THIS BOOK IS DEDICATED TO THE
MEMORY OF MY DEAR MOTHER
DORIS MIRIAM APPELQUIST
WHO ALWAYS ENCOURAGED ME TO
REACH FOR THE STARS

There is but one Earth, tiny and fragile, and one must get 100,000 miles away to appreciate fully one's good fortune in living on it.

– MICHAEL COLLINS –

*With the greatest leader above them,
people barely know one exists.
Next comes one whom they love and praise.
Next comes one whom they fear.
Next comes one whom they despise and defy.
When a leader trusts no one,
no one trusts him.
The great leader speaks little.
He never speaks carelessly.
He works without self-interest
and leaves no trace.
When all is finished, the people say
'We did it ourselves.'*

LAO TZU, *TAO TE CHING*, VERSE 17

TABLE OF CONTENTS

We choose to go to the Moon in this decade and do the other things, not because they are easy, but because they are hard.

JOHN F. KENNEDY
SEPTEMBER 1962

WE CHOOSE TO GO TO THE MOON

On the morning of Sunday July 20, 1969, when I was 11 years old, I asked my mother for a big favor: "Mom, I know it will be past my bedtime, but can I stay up tonight to watch our astronauts land on the Moon?" I was old enough by then to understand that I was growing up during tumultuous times. Although I was only a five-year-old kindergartner on November 22, 1963, I had a vivid recollection of the assassination of John Kennedy – he who only two years earlier had issued the original clarion call, challenging America to put a man on the Moon "before this decade is out." I heard my mother crying herself to sleep that night.

"Of course you can stay up and watch," she replied. "It will be a moment in history." This would also be a moment of profound inspiration and hope at the end of what had been a really hard time. In addition to the murder of a promising young president, the 1960s had seen the escalation of America's tragic and misguided involvement in faraway Vietnam; some but not enough progress in the Civil Rights movement; the heartbreaking assassinations of Dr. Martin Luther King, Jr., and then, just two months later, Robert F. Kennedy; widespread and deadly riots in our cities; and general political and social turmoil on a grand and disruptive scale. Despite all of this, somehow, imagining the possibility of reaching the Moon brought us together, even if only for a moment. It would be not just an American achievement, but an achievement for all people everywhere. If we were successful, it would truly represent a triumph of the human spirit.

By 1969, I was into organized sports and knew well the sensation of "butterflies" before an athletic contest. I can still remember the funny, queasy feeling that I and about 650 million other hopeful television viewers from around the world felt in the pits of our stomachs when we saw the grainy images of the spacecraft slowly descending to the Moon. We held our breath and whispered a collective prayer. Finally, we were jubilant when we heard Neil Armstrong's stirring declaration, "The *Eagle* has landed."

They set down on the lunar surface at 4:14 pm EST, with only 13 seconds of fuel remaining in the landing craft. At 10:56 pm EST, after several hours of preparation, Armstrong moved down the ladder onto the Moon: "That's one small step for [a] man, one giant leap for mankind" (more on those famous words later.) Buzz Aldrin followed his colleague to the surface 19 minutes later. The two intrepid astronauts spent a total of 21 hours and 36 minutes exploring the desolate place they had named Tranquility Base. They gathered rock samples, took photographs, communicated with Mission Control in Houston, spoke with President Richard Nixon, and planted an American flag. They then lifted off to rejoin Michael Collins, who was orbiting in the main ship, *Columbia*. They left the descent stage of the *Eagle* behind, and on it they placed a plaque that read, "Here men from the planet Earth first set foot upon the Moon July 1969, A.D. We came in peace for all mankind."

While I may have aspired to be an astronaut myself at age 11, that's not what transpired for me. Nevertheless, my life has been an interesting and varied journey. I have been extremely lucky. I grew up in the suburban Twin Cities of Minneapolis and St. Paul as the youngest of three children in a wonderful, loving family. We were solidly middle class. I served for three years as a Marine infantry officer after graduating from Carleton College with a B.A. in political science. My military service took me to both coasts of the United States and to the Far East. Back to the states again as a civilian, I attended graduate school at the University of Wisconsin – Madison, where I earned a combined juris doctor and master's degree in public policy and administration. I practiced law as a corporate litigator for a few years in the late 1980s, then embarked on a long business career.

I started by failing miserably, in entrepreneurship, as a restaurateur. I quickly found out what a tough business that is. My restaurant closed after just six months, and I was without a dollar in savings, bankrupt and unemployed. I have emphatically asserted ever since then that we learn more from our failures than from our victories – at least I have. My wife, Faith, worked hard to support our family (our daughter Anna was a toddler at the time – her sister Lucia came along two years later.) I eventually ended up working a combined 16 years in big-box retail for two excellent Minnesota companies, Target and Best Buy. I spent the last decade of my corporate career as a human resources generalist. Needless to say, I learned a lot about business, and life, during all those years.

While at Best Buy, in 2007, I tapped into my deep love of history and knowledge of the corporate world to develop an experiential leadership program based on visits to Gettysburg, Pennsylvania (site of a pivotal 1863 battle in the American Civil War) and Little Bighorn, Montana (site of Custer's Last Stand in 1876). Best Buy was highly supportive of this effort. I later added a program based on the incredible western journey of Lewis and Clark from 1804 to 1806. I and my colleague, Jack Uldrich, deliver that training out of Great Falls, Montana, and Skamania, Washington. In 2009, at the onset of the Great Recession, Best Buy offered a buyout to all of its corporate employees. I took a generous severance and formed my own company, now called Blue Knight Leadership, LLC. I weathered tough economic times, and have been doing leadership and business consulting, as well as taking corporate teams to historic venues, ever since. I enjoy being my own boss. They say that if you're going to work for an idiot, it might as well be yourself.

When I bring a team to these historic spots, we start with an afternoon session going through a series of preparatory exercises. My goal is to help business leaders understand how lessons from history can be extremely relevant in our day-to-day professional lives. The next day, after breakfast, I give a short lecture on the history of the places we will see firsthand. We then take a more-or-less chronological bus tour, stopping along the way to discuss the story of what happened at each location. We talk about many important leadership principles, with the primary goal of connecting history's myriad lessons back to our own lives.

The next morning, we spend a few more hours digesting and synthesizing what we experienced together. We formulate ideas, and develop tangible action steps for how we can take the new learning back to our places of work. We talk about what we will do differently going forward. We also discuss the enormity and the meaning of the epic events we have learned about. About half the time, someone sheds tears during this final session. Sometimes it is me. There is an undeniable heaviness to some of this subject matter, but I take great satisfaction in being able to share these unforgettable historical episodes with my teams. We need to better understand America's past, all the good, the bad and the ugly of it. In the end, people almost uniformly come away genuinely moved and changed by what they have seen and heard. I know this is true, because many of them tell me so, sometimes years later. My heart sings when that happens.

I am most richly blessed, for I love what I do.

Over the years, I have come to the conclusion that there are six "leadership dimensions" (this is what I call them - we could also label them leadership principles, attributes, behaviors, qualities, skills, etc.) that truly matter. They are not original to me; I did not conjure them up. There are many other dimensions and qualities that we could talk about. But based upon my deep, lifelong study of history, and more than four decades of real-world experience in the military, law and business, these are the timeless dimensions that have come to resonate with me. Here are the six things that truly great leaders, no matter what era they live in, consistently do well:

> » Great leaders create common purpose.
> » Great leaders build strong relationships and trust.
> » Great leaders communicate clearly and share information.
> » Great leaders seek self-knowledge and learning.
> » Great leaders demonstrate energy and passion.
> » Great leaders make good decisions.

Common purpose is incredibly important - there is a reason that I list it first among the leadership dimensions. No team can be successful over time without a unified common purpose. I think that leaders and organizations sometimes get too wound up and unnecessarily sidetracked when it comes to nomenclature. People will inquire with me as to the difference between common purpose and vision, or common purpose and mission. The argument about terminology confuses people and misses the main point. Regardless of whether we use the term vision, mission, goal, strategy, identity, or purpose, what matters most is that the people in your organization understand the single compelling idea that moves the organization forward.

The common purpose should be succinct, memorable and measureable. Leadership needs to communicate the common purpose, again and again. Not everyone has to agree with the common purpose, but everyone needs to understand what it is. If the people in your organization do not know what they are supposed to be doing in their jobs, and why, then you are without a common purpose. Further, if you have a clearly stated common purpose, but people do not understand how what they do every day contributes to that common purpose, then you have a serious disconnect. Common purpose may be thrust upon the organization based on external events or market conditions. Some organizations only discover their common purpose over time. No matter the origin, only organizations with a clear, compelling common purpose are able to evolve, maintain focus, and effectively navigate their way through constantly changing circumstances. Today, as we try to emerge from a great and tragic pandemic, common purpose is more critical than ever.

Long-term success is also impossible without a foundation of strong, trusting relationships. I have been a part of teams where mistrust ran rampant and relationships were strained – or even nonexistent. Those teams did not function well. But trust is a tricky and difficult thing. You cannot simply say to someone, "Please trust me." Trust must be earned, based upon actions rather than words. This takes time, even for the best of leaders. Once trust is earned and strong relationships established, all things become possible. Great leaders know this and so they patiently strive to build and maintain a culture where people care about each other. They set the example, demonstrating that they themselves truly care about their people. They take time to get to know each team member, both personally and professionally. They understand what makes each person tick, and they adjust their leadership approach accordingly.

The best leaders also encourage a culture of frequent team interaction, which builds comradery. They have a sense of humor and foster an environment where it is okay to engage in a bit of tomfoolery, have fun and laugh, because this builds team spirit. Great leaders set high standards and provide clear direction. Then they get out of the way, trusting their people to do their jobs and achieve the organization's goals. In my experience, trusting, caring relationships are an essential attribute of all high-performing teams.

If I had to identify the number one problem and frustration that bedevils the business teams I work with, it is communication. Even though today's communications technology is highly sophisticated, that does not always translate into better communication. I have seen communication in the modern corporate world get just as god-awful screwed up as it did on several occasions at the battles of Gettysburg and the Little Bighorn.

The best leaders are outstanding communicators. They put a strong emphasis on and take pride in this skill. They ensure that their teams understand their message by using multiple channels and erring on the side of over-communication. They are sensitive to their audience and adjust communication as necessary. They tell the truth, even if is unpleasant. Sometimes they are blunt. Interestingly, I have found another common trait among leaders who are superb communicators: they are excellent storytellers. They understand the power of a vivid, memorable story to make a point and motivate people to act. Finally, my mother told me I have one mouth and two ears for a reason (she really did.) Perhaps the most important communication skill is listening. Great leaders sincerely seek to understand, ask questions, demand honest feedback, shut their mouths, and then listen carefully to what people are telling them.

In that spirit, when asked what he believed was his finest leadership characteristic, John Kennedy answered, "Curiosity." Great leaders are desperately curious about the world. They are intense learners, always asking questions, full of wonder, always seeking new knowledge. The best that I have ever known were all voracious readers. These leaders demonstrate humility in that they deliberately surround themselves with people who know more than they do. Then they endeavor to learn from those people, and to allow those people to use their unique skills to help the team reach its goals. Great leaders are also willing to look in the mirror and be honest about what they see. They possess outstanding self-knowledge and emotional intelligence. They are often their own worst critics. They admit what they don't know, but then strive to find the answers. Great leaders make constant adjustments and improvements based upon what they learn.

When I teach the leadership dimension that I call energy and passion, I sometimes get blank stares from a handful of people in my audience. I generally discover that it's not that these folks don't believe in the importance of this trait, it's that they simply don't think that they have it. "I'm not a loud, outgoing, rah-rah kind of leader," they will lament. Indeed, it is said that at least one-third of the general population is introverted – including lots of introverts in leadership roles. But one does not need to be an extrovert to show energy and passion. Some of the quiet people I know are among the most energetic and passionate leaders I have ever met. Bud Grant was the long-time head coach of my beloved Minnesota Vikings football team. He took the Vikes to the Super Bowl four times in the 1960s and '70s (lost them all – that is another story altogether – no time in this book). Bud was among the lowest-key individuals you could ever encounter. It seemed sometimes that he barely had a pulse. Yet he was an intense competitor, tough as nails, a great teacher, and a superb leader who inspired his guys to try to win every time they took the field. His philosophy was "don't get too high when things go well, and don't get too low when they go badly."

As Bud Grant well knew, energy and passion can be demonstrated in countless different ways, by any leader, be they introvert or extrovert. Do you work hard? Are you passionate about your profession? Do you strive to be the best? Do you take time to get to know your people? Are you a learner who constantly seeks new knowledge? Do you teach what you know? Do you set high standards and inspire your team to meet them? If yes, then you are an energetic and passionate leader.

Decision making is the final of the six leadership dimensions. I list it last not because it is the least important, but because in many ways it is the paramount leadership skill. You can be doing all of the other things very well, but if you are constantly making one stupid decision after another, you will not last long in a leadership role in any organization that I know of. One need not be perfect, but one must be consistent and learn from mistakes.

The best leaders don't keep making the same dumb choices over and over. They gather all the relevant information that time allows to help in their decision making. They consult with their team, use their expert resources well, and think things through. But the information they receive is hardly ever perfect or complete. So they have developed a sixth sense of when to pull the trigger. Their timing is generally impeccable. They enjoy the benefit of having had many at-bats; even then, sometimes they strike out. If they make a mistake they admit it, take responsibility, learn from it, and lead their teams forward. Consistently exercising sound judgment and making good decisions is the most critical, and difficult, thing that leaders get paid to do.

Occasionally, I will get pushback on these dimensions to the effect that they are so exceedingly simple as to not be worth talking about. *Everyone understands that these are the fundamental things that good leaders must do, right? Don't waste my time.* My response is yes, these are clear, easily grasped principles. But are you any good at them? Are you doing these things well? The number of leaders I have ever encountered - myself included - who are highly proficient in all six of these dimensions is exactly zero. Comprehension and execution are two entirely different concepts – one is easy, the other hard. So the work continues.

I first outlined the six leadership dimensions in a book I wrote in 2010 called *Sacred Ground: Leadership Lessons from Gettysburg & the Little Bighorn.* Over the years, that book has served as the companion volume to the experiential learning adventures I lead at those hallowed fields. I ask teams to read the book before our events – it gives them necessary historical context and also provides relevant examples from modern business scenarios of how the dimensions play out in real life. Again, the objective is to emphasize how lessons from history can be relevant to our own professional journeys.

Obviously, my adherence to the importance of those dimensions has not wavered in over a decade. It never will. I had seriously considered in recent times going back and updating *Sacred Ground,* not to change the leadership dimensions but to provide more current case studies and examples of the dimensions in action. Some of my stories from that book are old and stale: Jack Welch at General Electric, Meg Whitman at eBay, Magic Johnson Enterprises, etc. I needed to "rocket" into the 21st century.

In 2019, based upon my lifelong fascination with the American space program, I developed the idea of designing an experiential curriculum centered on the Apollo missions. This event would be run in Houston, Texas out of the Johnson Space Center, an absolutely magnificent facility and a true national treasure. I traveled to Houston twice and spent considerable time checking everything out. I was all set to go, had finalized the course design, had a couple of pilot teams lined up to attend, and then the pandemic hit. So, like everyone else, I was stymied and delayed. It dawned on me that the Apollo program needed a companion volume just like the battlefield events, and that a pandemic would be a good time to research and write. It further came to me that rather than revise *Sacred Ground,* I could simply write an all-new book, using the same enduring dimensions, but with a different historical scenario and all-new case studies. And so you hold in your hands *Earthrise: Leadership Lessons from the Apollo Space Missions.*

Simply put, the question this book seeks to answer is what leadership lessons can we glean from the Apollo spaceflights? I have chosen to focus on three missions: Apollo 8 (the first orbiting of the moon, at Christmas-time in 1968); Apollo 11 ("one small step..." in July 1969); and Apollo 13 ("Houston, we've had a problem..." in April 1970). I will attach two of the leadership dimensions to each of the missions and explain how those dimensions played themselves out. Apollo 8 abounded with lessons around self-knowledge and learning as well as energy and passion. Apollo 11 demonstrated common purpose and decision making in action. Apollo 13 reflected the importance of relationships, trust and communication. I will also provide two modern-day, (mostly) 21st-century-current case studies for each dimension to further cement understanding of these critical leadership lessons.

In all of the historical experiential programs that I lead, including the new Apollo program, I am keenly cognizant that, depending on one's point of view and how the material is taught, these are predominantly stories about the experiences, achievements, trials and tribulations of white men. I am also acutely aware that, in this day and age, with so much work to be done by all of us around racial and gender equality and social justice, a lot of people are sick of these "white man" stories.

With that in mind, I have always focused at Gettysburg on the fact that less than 160 years ago, in the United States of America, almost four million human beings lived in bondage. I challenge people to think about that - it is incredible and depressing to contemplate. Slavery is what the Civil War was about. It was an epic, bloody contest to determine what kind of a nation we would be. Did the words "all men are created equal" from our Declaration of Independence really have meaning, or were they just words? Ultimately, the union was preserved and slavery was abolished; but in a very real sense we are still fighting the Civil War to this day. The Gettysburg story, to me, is just as much about the historical experience of Black Americans, the evil of the institution of slavery, and the struggle for freedom and equality as it is about leadership or military strategy and tactics.

In Montana, for both the Lewis and Clark and Little Bighorn programs, I emphasize the Native American history and point of view. I figure if I am going to be accused of bias, I want to be accused of bias in favor of the Native perspective. It seems these stories are almost always told from the white culture's vantage point. They represent the traditional saga of America's gallant westward expansion, with primitive, savage Indian tribes standing in the way of inevitable white progress. Instead, I challenge my teams to imagine how things must have looked and felt to Native Americans. They faced an onslaught of disease, displacement and genocide brought by the white man. I call upon folks to "Look East," and imagine how dramatically things were going to change for the West's original inhabitants after living and surviving successfully for six hundred generations (that's right, archaeological evidence tells us that Indians tribes have occupied the American West for at least 12,000 years, and probably longer) in their cherished ancestral lands. Again, it is a mind-bender for my predominantly white, privileged audiences.

For the amazing Apollo story that follows, I will highlight the team nature of the endeavor. Indeed, literally hundreds of thousands of people, from every different background, contributed to the effort to put astronauts on the Moon. The story that is so well told in the book and movie entitled *Hidden Figures* of the group of Black women, brilliant mathematicians all, who helped America win the space race (more on this in Chapter One) is just one poignant example. I will also strive in the case studies to present diverse examples. After all, great leaders can and do come from every place on the spectrum of God's vast rainbow coalition of humanity.

Now, let's all go to the Moon together, shall we?

Jeff Appelquist
Minneapolis, March 2022

PART ONE

OVERVIEW & APOLLO 8

*Get the girl to check the numbers.
If she says the numbers are good,
I am ready to go.*

ASTRONAUT JOHN GLENN,
AS QUOTED IN MARGOT LEE SHETTERLY'S
BOOK *HIDDEN FIGURES*

CHAPTER ONE

OVERVIEW: SPACE RACE

Katherine Goble Johnson died on February 24th, 2020, at the age of 101. By the end of her long, eventful life she had earned numerous honorary doctorates, and received the Presidential Medal of Freedom from Barack Obama – when she was a sprightly 97. She had a building at the National Aeronautics and Space Administration (NASA) facility in Hampton, Virginia, named after her. A popular book and movie told her amazing story.

She was a mathematical genius who had graduated from high school at age 14 and college at 18. She absorbed and mastered all of the mathematical subjects that anyone had ever been able to teach her. She was also fascinated by astronomy. In 1953, in recognition of her talent, she was plucked away from the computer pool at the Langley Aeronautical Laboratory – later to become part of NASA - to assist the male engineers of the Flight Research Division.

But Katherine Johnson had a difficult road ahead, for not only was she new in her role, and a woman, she was also Black. The segregated pool that she became a part of was called "Colored Computing." She nevertheless labored on, developing special skill in the area of calculating flight trajectories for spacecraft, based on precise launch windows. Her objective was to make sure that a module could leave Earth's orbit and return safely home again. Her work was accomplished with paper, pencil and brainpower. Her dependability became so widely respected that prior to astronaut John Glenn's first orbital flight in 1962, he insisted that "the girl" (then 43 years old) manually double-check the electronic computer's numbers. Only then would he confidently embark on his historic mission.

Katherine Johnson was one of a group of a dozen or so Black women, known as the "computers in skirts," who persevered with determination, energy and dignity against the pervasive gender and racial discrimination of that era. Katherine's career at Langley and NASA lasted 33 years. An obituary in the February 29, 2020, issue of *The Economist* said of Katherine, "... for her, the work had been its own reward. She just did her job, enjoying every minute. The struggles of being both Black and a woman were shrugged away. Do your best, she always said. Love what you do. Be constantly curious. And learn that it is not dumb to ask a question, it is dumb not to ask it." In the end, she had only passion for her job and positive remembrances about what had been achieved: "I loved every single day of it. There wasn't one day when I wasn't excited to go to work."

It is estimated that 400,000 people, both inside and outside of NASA, contributed over time to the success of the Moon landing. As Apollo 11 returned to Earth in July 1969, Neil Armstrong expressed his gratitude: "We would like to give a special thanks to all those Americans who built the spacecraft, who did the construction, the design, the tests, and put their hearts and all their abilities into those crafts. To those people tonight, we give a special thank-you. And to all the other people that are listening and watching tonight, God bless you. Good night from Apollo 11."

The first and perhaps most important leadership lesson of the Apollo missions is to demonstrate the power of what can be attained by a diverse team of talented people, dedicated to a common purpose, working together hand-in-hand.

● ❱ ❱ ❭ ○ ❬ ❬ ❬ ●

On July 29, 1958, President Dwight D. Eisenhower signed into law a federal statute, the National Aeronautics and Space Act. The law laid out the parameters for the creation of a space agency called the National Aeronautics and Space Administration. NASA was unique in that it would be entirely controlled by civilians, without direct military involvement or oversight. NASA absorbed the $100 million budget and 8,000 employees of its predecessor office, the National Advisory Committee for Aeronautics. A separate innovation center, the secretive Advanced Research Projects Agency, had already been established in February 1958, for purposes of studying military applications of space technology. Nevertheless, Eisenhower, former five-star general though he was, had long harbored distrust for what he later characterized as the "military-industrial complex." Civilian scientists and engineers would therefore reign supreme at NASA, and they would channel their endeavors for peaceful purposes.

The United States, Great Britain and the Soviet Union formed a successful, if wary, allied partnership to defeat Germany in the Second World War. Soon upon vanquishing the Nazi enemy in 1945, and the launching of two U.S. nuclear strikes to force a Japanese surrender, relations between America and the Soviets began to fracture. In 1949, the Russians successfully detonated an atomic weapon, so there were now two members of the nuclear club. Cooperation swiftly gave way to mistrust and bitter rivalry, particularly in military and scientific matters. The emerging superpowers both looked to the heavens, and the potential for conquering outer space to gain a national security advantage.

America's worst fears were realized when on October 4, 1957, the Russians launched Sputnik 1. Sputnik was compact – roughly the size of a basketball – and weighed only 183 pounds. It was the first manmade satellite to orbit the Earth; a complete circumnavigation took 98 minutes. Sputnik gave off radio signals heard by amateur operators all over the globe, and it continued on its path for 1,440 orbital trips and 43 million miles before its batteries died, just over three weeks after launch. This event caused an upheaval in the ranks of America's military and governmental establishment. The "Space Race" was on, and the U.S. was losing.

Prominent Democratic politicians spoke up, arguing vociferously that the U.S. and, more specifically, the Republican Eisenhower Administration, had been caught badly off guard. Two of the most vocal were Senators John F. Kennedy of Massachusetts and Majority Leader Lyndon B. Johnson of Texas – both of whom were vying for the Democratic presidential nomination in 1960. Kennedy expressly criticized what he characterized as Eisenhower's lackadaisical attitude concerning this grave blow to American prestige and national security. Johnson captured the fears of countless Americans when he said, "Now the Communists have established a foothold in outer space… Soon, the Russians will be dropping bombs on us from space like kids dropping rocks onto cars from freeway overpasses." Johnson wrote of the Sputnik moment later, in his memoirs: "In the Open West you learn to live closely with the sky. It is part of your life. But now, somehow, in some new way, the sky seemed almost alien. I also remember the profound shock of realizing that it might be possible for another nation to achieve technological superiority over this great country of ours."

By the middle 1950s, both the American and Soviet militaries had come to the realization that the strategy of delivering atomic weapons via standard bombers - such as the B-29 Superfortresses that dropped the payloads which decimated the

Japanese cities of Hiroshima and Nagasaki - was outmoded. Technology had moved forward, and the new delivery system would need to be a rocket. The Nazis, in no small part thanks to the scientific genius of Werner von Braun, had developed the V-2 rocket system. These missiles devastated targets in London and elsewhere in the fall of 1944. The V-2 had a range of only 200 miles, was inaccurate, and came along too late in the war to change Adolf Hitler's fortunes. But the technology held vast potential. In the decade after the war, both the Americans and Soviets worked to develop missiles capable of hitting targets thousands of miles away. And it was, after all, a missile that had launched Sputnik into space.

One month after Sputnik 1 completed its orbital run, the Soviets launched Sputnik 2. For the first time a living creature – a dog named Laika – was sent into orbit. Alas, Laika died during the flight due to overheating, but the Russians had again proven that they were ahead in the Space Race. America labored desperately to respond with a launch of its own. A series of embarrassing setbacks ensued. A rocket called Vanguard, with a grapefruit-sized satellite attached, blew up ingloriously moments after liftoff in December 1957. The failed project came to be dubbed by world media variously as "Flopnik," "Kaputnik," and "Stayputnik." The Soviets reveled in America's humiliation. Finally, on January 31, 1958, Explorer I launched successfully aboard a Juno rocket. It was the first of more than 90 spacecraft in the Explorer Series. Explorer 1 weighed just over 30 pounds, and effectively transmitted data back to Earth for four months until its batteries expired. A satellite called Vanguard 1 launched six weeks after Explorer 1. Though it was derisively nicknamed "the grapefruit" by Soviet Premier Nikita Krushchev, the Vanguard satellite remains in orbit to this day.

NASA finally became fully operational in October 1958. Two months later came the announcement of Project Mercury, which would pursue the mission of launching a man into outer space and returning him and his spacecraft safely back to Earth. Without Project Mercury, the Apollo missions would never have happened. The Mercury leadership team would seek to recruit seven brave astronauts – "star voyagers" - to accomplish this unprecedented goal.

In April 1959, after an arduous selection process, NASA administrator Thomas Keith Glennan announced the seven military pilots who had been chosen as the Mercury astronauts: Malcolm Scott Carpenter (Navy); Leroy Gordon Cooper Jr. (Air Force); John Herschel Glenn Jr. (Marine Corps); Virgil Ivan "Gus" Grissom (Air Force); Walter Marty Schirra Jr. (Navy); Alan Bartlett Shepard Jr. (Navy); and Donald Kent "Deke" Slayton (Air Force). They ranged in age from 32 (Cooper) to 37 (Glenn). No one among them weighed more than 180 pounds or was taller than 5'11" – they were compact, as a pilot should be and an astronaut would have to be. They were uniformly smart, fit, talented, tough, and hungry for glory. Each had swagger, in his own way. These men, who would soon catapult to fame, were the "Mercury Seven."

From an initial pool of 110 would-be astronauts, and after a series of grueling physical, mental and psychological tests, the final seven emerged. The NASA selection committee had established a hard-and-fast criteria that all of the astronauts must be military test pilots with extensive experience in high-performance aircraft. This rule prevented people such as future Apollo hero Neil Armstrong from even being considered (Armstrong, in turn, had no interest in joining Project Mercury.)

The pilots-only restriction also obviously precluded women from consideration for the program, as no woman during that era was a military test pilot. But a privately funded experiment led by William Randolph Lovelace, chairman of NASA's Special Advisory Committee on Life Science, put 13 American women through the very same battery of tests that the Mercury Seven underwent. These women not only passed those tests, but in some cases surpassed the performance of their male counterparts. They were never formally a part of NASA, nor did any of them ever fly in outer space (with one exception, to be described in the Conclusion). Later, some of these first female astronaut trainees, who became known as the "Mercury 13", lobbied Congress for women to be included in the astronaut program. Nevertheless, although the Soviets put a woman into orbit in 1963, it would not be until 20 years later that the first American woman, Dr. Sally Ride, would go into outer space.

Once selected, the Mercury Seven embarked on an intense regimen in preparation for the missions to come. They trained in basic astronautical science, systems, spacecraft control, environmental familiarization, egress, and survival. A great deal of thought and labor had gone into the design of the spacecraft that would carry the men into orbit. Robert Gilruth was an aerospace engineer and the first director of NASA's Manned Spacecraft Center. In the book *Apollo Expeditions to the Moon*, he described how the design process evolved: "Most of the effort in the early days had been directed toward hypersonic gliders, or winged vehicles, that would fly at high Mach numbers and perhaps even into orbit. But our views were changing, and Harvey Allen of the Ames Laboratory was the first... to propose a blunt body for flying man into space. He suggested a sphere to enclose the man and said, 'you just throw it,' meaning of course launch it into space with a rocket. In March 1958, Max Faget presented a paper that was to be a milestone in spacecraft design. His paper proposed a simple blunt-body vehicle that would reenter the atmosphere without reaching heating rates or accelerations that would be dangerous to man. He showed that small retrorockets were adequate to initiate reentry from orbit. He suggested the use of parachutes for final descent, and small attitude jets for controlling the capsule in orbit during retro fire and reentry."

Gilruth readily acknowledged the unfortunate fallout that resulted. He explained: "This concept of the Mercury capsule and, indeed, the whole plan for putting man into space was remarkable in its elegant simplicity. Yet it's very daring and unconventional approach made it the subject of considerable controversy. Some people felt that such a means for flying a man in space was only a stunt. The blunt body in particular was under fire since it was such a radical departure from the airplane. It was called by its opponents 'the man in the can,' and the pilot was termed only a medical specimen."

The idea of the astronaut as not a pilot at all, but rather merely a passenger in a tiny capsule that would be catapulted into space took a powerful hold. Neil Armstrong, for one, who was at the time a civilian test pilot for NASA, much preferred the cutting edge work he was doing than the prospect of sitting helpless in a blunt body and being thrown into orbit by a rocket. But the impression of 'man in a can' would soon change, and the Mercury Seven would demonstrate their fortitude beyond a doubt. They did indeed possess what author Tom Wolfe termed, "The Right Stuff."

Russian cosmonaut Yuri Gagarin became the first human being in space when he completed a single Earth orbit in 108 minutes on April 12, 1961. Three weeks later, on May 5th, Alan Shepard became the first American in space. He made a 15-minute suborbital trip, riding aboard the *Freedom 7* capsule. The launch of the Redstone rocket had been delayed that morning by technical challenges, and Shepard was forced to endure four hours on his back, waiting for liftoff. At one point, he asked for and received permission to urinate in his space suit, such was the length of the delay and the resulting fullness in his bladder. Finally, in a moment of deep frustration, Shepard succinctly expressed the sentiments of all Americans who were anxious to catch and surpass the Soviets in the Space Race. As NASA engineers continued to dither, further extending his ordeal, Shepard famously suggested, "Why don't you fix your little problem and light this candle?!" They lit the candle. The U.S. Navy retrieved Shepard and his capsule from the Atlantic Ocean, near the Bahamas, and he returned home a national hero, honored by John Kennedy in a White House ceremony.

Kennedy had recently made a decision that America needed to set a big, audacious, long-term objective in order to reestablish U.S. scientific and technological superiority over the U.S.S.R. He instructed a small group of aides, "I want some answers. Ask the janitor over there if you have to. But I want to know how and when we can get to the moon." When the president consulted with his scientific experts, they told him that the race to the Moon would take a decade, and that it would cost the astronomical sum of $40 billion. Kennedy was undeterred. Accordingly, on May 25, 1961, 20 days after Shepard's history-making flight, in a speech before a joint session of Congress, Kennedy declared, "I believe that this nation should commit itself to achieving the goal, before this decade is out, of landing a man on the Moon and returning him safely to the Earth. No single space project in this period will be more impressive to mankind, or more important to the long-range exploration of space, and none will be so difficult or expensive to accomplish." At the time of Kennedy's ringing call to action, America had a sum total of 15 minutes of experience in space. Gene Kranz, then a young man working on the Mercury project who would later become the flight director for Apollo 11, said, "To those of us who had watched our rockets keel over, spin out of control, or blow up, the idea of putting a man on the Moon seemed almost too breathtakingly ambitious."

The next Mercury mission was a near tragedy. Gus Grissom flew the *Liberty Bell 7* and, like Shepard, spent 15 minutes in space. This capsule had a newly installed, explosively-activated side hatch door which blew out early (whether on its own or through the fault of a nervous Grissom became a controversial question), causing the capsule to sink. Grissom escaped *Liberty Bell 7* and bobbed in the Atlantic Ocean for a few moments before he was saved from drowning by Navy rescuers.

On February 20, 1962, John Glenn became the first American to orbit the Earth. The Atlas launch vehicle threw *Friendship 7* into space, and in just under five hours Glenn orbited the planet three times. Subsequent Project Mercury flights focused on operational research, with a particular emphasis on discovering the impact of spaceflight on the human body. In May, Scott Carpenter flew *Aurora 7* as he replicated Glenn's mission, spending an equal amount of time in space and confirming no serious ill effects on the body.

On a blistering hot September 12, 1962, in a memorable speech at Rice University Stadium in Houston, Texas, John Kennedy elaborated on his vision of a moonshot: "But why, some say, the moon? And they may well ask: Why climb the highest mountain? Why 35 years ago fly the Atlantic? Why does Rice play Texas? We choose to go to the moon in this decade and do the other things, not because they are easy, but because they are hard – because that goal will serve to organize and measure the best of our energies and skills – because that challenge is one we are willing to accept, one we are unwilling to postpone, and one we intend to win."

Now more than ever, the remainder of Project Mercury became a quest to determine how much time a human being could spend in space without damaging physical consequences to the body. On October 3, Wally Schirra flew *Sigma 7*, spending nine hours in space while orbiting Earth six times. In Mercury's grand finale, Gordon Cooper rode the *Faith 7* spacecraft for 34 hours – an expanse of time that would have been inconceivable when Shepard first launched in May 1961. This mission convinced scientists that man could safely fly for more than a full day in outer space (Cooper further proved that the Mercury Seven had the right stuff – as he sat flat on his back atop the Atlas rocket, waiting for blast off, he promptly fell asleep, to the great wonder and amusement of the team in Mission Control.)

Director Robert Gilruth summarized the importance of Project Mercury to the ultimate goal of reaching the moon: "We were to learn much from the flights of Glenn, Carpenter, Schirra, and Cooper that helped us in planning for the lunar program... The exposure of man to zero gravity in these early manned flights was perhaps among the greatest medical experiments of all time. All the Mercury astronauts found the weightless state no particular problem. All returned to Earth with no medical difficulties whatever... It now became simply a question of how long man could withstand weightlessness, and detailed medical measurements were made to cast light on how the body compensated for the new environment. Zero gravity produced some problems in locomotion and habitability, but not in man himself. We believed that even the longest flights of the future would probably require only methods of keeping the human body properly exercised and nourished in order to prevent a different reaction on returning to the gravity of Earth."

The learning from Project Mercury had been profound. But there was still work to do before any realistic chance of a successful moon landing. Project Gemini, formally conceived in January 1962, bridged the gap between Mercury and the Apollo Moon program. With the Apollo spacecraft still under design, there was a clear need to create an intermediate vehicle. The overall purpose of Gemini was to investigate critical situations in actual flight that would be encountered on the Apollo missions. The Gemini capsule was built to accommodate more than one astronaut on longer voyages. The spacecraft carried an onboard propulsion system that allowed for maneuvering in orbit. Of the various procedures that would be required to enable travel to the moon, none was more critical than techniques of rendezvous and docking. Accordingly, the Gemini spacecraft had a guidance and navigation system and rendezvous radar that enabled astronauts to dock in space with an Agena target vehicle.

There were 10 manned missions in the Gemini program between March 1965 and November 1966. The result was 2,000 invaluable man-hours in space that confirmed the feasibility of the precise maneuvers that Apollo would require. The team mastered rendezvous and docking procedures. Gemini missions went to altitudes of more than 800 nautical miles and extended durations in orbit with no ill effects on the health of the astronauts. On the Gemini 4 mission, astronaut Ed White became the first American to walk in space. The Gemini 6 mission, manned by future Apollo astronauts Frank Borman and Jim Lovell, set records with nearly two weeks in flight, five million miles traveled, and 206 Earth orbits.

In short, Gemini gave NASA the confidence to successfully conduct complex space operations. The team in Mission Control gained essential operational experience that would allow for superb flight management. Public interest in and support of the space program remained incredibly strong. The effort had the enthusiastic backing of national political leadership, from President Kennedy on down. With the conclusion of the final mission, Gemini 12, the stage was set and anticipation was high for the debut of Apollo.

In the beginning God created the heaven and the earth. And the earth was without form and void; and darkness was upon the face of the deep.

**GENESIS 1, HOLY BIBLE,
KING JAMES VERSION**

CHAPTER TWO

APOLLO 8: EARTHRISE

Sometimes out of profound and tragic failure comes insight, learning and progress – painfully-won progress, but progress nonetheless. In January of 1967, America appeared on track to achieve JFK's audacious vision of a Moon landing by the end of the decade. Kennedy did not live to see his dream fulfilled, but the goal seemed tantalizingly within reach. For the first time, America had pulled ahead in the Space Race. Rapid technological advancements from the Mercury and Gemini programs positioned NASA to confidently schedule the first manned, earth-orbit Apollo flight for February of '67. Three astronauts would journey aboard what was known as the AS-204 mission (later dubbed Apollo 1): command pilot and former Mercury veteran Gus Grissom, age 40; senior pilot Ed White (the first man to walk in space), age 36; and rookie pilot Roger Chaffee, 31. But on the evening of January 27, high atop an immense Saturn 1B booster rocket at the Pad 34 launch complex, hard on the Atlantic Ocean at Cape Kennedy, Florida, all of the soaring hopes and dreams came tumbling catastrophically back to Earth.

"How are we going to get to the moon if we can't talk between three buildings?" Gus Grissom remained calm, but he was unmistakably irritated. Even among the legendary Mercury Seven, Grissom stood out: a fierce, tough, competitive, works-hard-plays-hard kind of guy. Though he was short and compact, he was not a man to be trifled with. When Gus spoke, people listened. He had been an elite fighter and test pilot. A senior veteran of both Mercury and Gemini space flights, Grissom had aspirations of being the first man to set foot upon the Moon; had circumstances turned out differently he might well have been. For months he had been monitoring progress and working to ensure that the Apollo program succeeded. His exasperation grew as a seemingly endless series of engineering problems kept cropping up. He pushed for solutions based on his long experience, but no one seemed to hear him.

The Apollo 1 command module, produced by North American Aviation in Downey, California, contained serious flaws. When the contractor delivered the spacecraft to Cape Kennedy in August 1966, there were still 113 major engineering changes due to be completed upon arrival. An additional 623 technical modifications were identified and completed after delivery. Among other major concerns were the copious amount of flammable materials and the pure oxygen atmosphere in the cockpit. Even the command module simulator at Cape Kennedy had dozens of bugs. To make a point, Grissom had picked a gigantic lemon from a tree in his Texas back yard and hung it in mockery on the outside of the simulator. Grissom well understood that technical challenges were to be fully expected with any engineering project of such complexity and magnitude. As much as anyone, he wanted the February launch to take place on schedule. He was frustrated nonetheless.

The simulated countdown on January 27 was a routine test. There was minimal danger; the rocket contained no fuel. This would be what was known as an "unplugged" check of systems and procedures, while running as closely as possible to actual flight conditions. A simulated launch would be a key part of the test. But from the very start, when the crew entered the capsule around 1 pm, things went wrong. Grissom immediately identified an odor in the breathing oxygen that he described as smelling like "sour buttermilk." The ensuing investigation resulted in a delay of more than an hour (this glitch was later found to be unrelated to the disaster that unfolded.) Additional delays came about due to disrupted communications from a microphone that could not be turned off. At around 6:30 pm, when Grissom wondered aloud about reaching the Moon when the team couldn't even talk to each other on the ground, another crew member said, "They can't hear a word you're saying." "Jesus Christ," muttered Grissom, then he repeated his question. One minute later, there occurred a surge in readings of the spacecraft's alternating current voltage, which indicated a short circuit in a bundle of wiring.

The renowned Gene Kranz, a NASA flight director, recounted what happened next in his memoir, *Failure Is Not an Option*: "A brief voice report jolted the launch and flight teams. It was perhaps the defining moment in our race to get to the Moon.

After this, nothing would ever be quite the same again. *'Fire!' 'We've got fire in the cock-pit!' 'We've got a bad fire... get us out. We're burning up...'* The last sound was a scream, shrill and brief. The elapsed time of the crew report: twelve seconds... There would be no final agreement as to who in the Apollo spacecraft shouted what. But even today, just reading the words on paper is chilling."

The effort to extricate the doomed astronauts was immediate and heroic, but futile. Emergency procedures calling for Ed White, physically powerful man though he was, to open the inward-releasing hatch from inside the capsule could not be accomplished because interior atmospheric pressure exceeded exterior pressure. Under normal circumstances, opening the hatch from the outside required ratchets and could be completed in 90 seconds. But billowing flames and smoke hurled ground personnel violently backward as they rushed to the rescue and kept them at bay for five minutes. Some technicians passed out from the fumes. By the time the searing hatch was finally opened, the fire had stanched itself from atmospheric air rushing into the command module through the ruptured hull. The astronauts were dead, asphyxiated by toxic fumes and overcome by heat and flames.

Gene Kranz eloquently summarized the deep sadness of this event and the task that loomed ahead: "In these harrowing days that followed there was no way to comprehend the loss of Grissom, White, and Chafee. If there was something that could be retrieved from this tragedy, it was the evidence – it was right there in front of us on Pad 34. We had a chance to discover the cause of the fire before another spacecraft was put at risk... The fire did something else. It reminded the American public that men would die in our efforts to explore the heavens. It recreated the tension and uncertainty of the early flights of Shepard, Grissom, and Glenn. The Russians worked in secret, but the entire world could watch our flights on television. Success had become almost routine for us... until now. The country had gotten complacent."

Frank Borman and Ed White were as close as brothers. Like White, Borman was a West Point-trained aviator and astronaut for whom family always came first. Both men were straight arrows, honest and patriotic. Their wives had become extremely close friends, and the two families frequently vacationed together. When Borman received the heartbreaking news from NASA astronaut manager Deke Slayton that

White and the others had been killed, Borman was stunned. Slayton further informed Borman, who was home in Houston at the time, that he was needed at the Cape as soon as possible, as he had been appointed to the committee that would investigate the accident. Borman's status as the only astronaut on the committee spoke to the high regard in which he was held.

Borman's first task was to supervise disassembly of the burned-out Apollo 1 spacecraft to determine the exact cause of the fire. He spent the next two months inside the charred, nightmarish remains of the cabin to review design flaws and work to suggest solutions. With the Apollo program suspended, the NASA review board completed its work. Ultimately, the committee identified six contributing causes to the fire: a sealed, pressurized cabin with an oxygen atmosphere; highly combustible materials inside the cabin; sensitive wiring connected to spacecraft power; a corrosive, combustible coolant in the plumbing; poor capability for the crew to escape; and inadequate emergency and medical response capability. Fixes were put into place to make subsequent Apollo flights as safe as humanly possible.

Naturally, there were many prominent voices that called for quitting the Moon program. But others, including NASA personnel at every level, were determined to proceed on. In April 1967, Frank Borman testified before Congress. As quoted in Robert Kurson's book, *Rocket Men: The Daring Odyssey of Apollo 8 and the Astronauts Who Made Man's First Journey to the Moon*, Borman told the skeptical congressional investigators, "We are trying to tell you that we are confident in our management, and in our engineering, and in ourselves. I think the question is really: Are you confident in us?" At the end of the hearings, Borman declared, "Let's stop the witch hunt and get on with it." Congress ultimately agreed. NASA continued on its mission.

Subsequent to the Apollo 1 catastrophe, the nomenclature of the missions changed. There was no Apollo 2 or 3, and the next launch, Apollo 4, would be what was known as a Type-A unmanned flight. This mission would be the first test of the Saturn V rocket that would ultimately propel astronauts to the Moon. The Saturn V is arguably the most amazing rocket ever created. Werner von Braun (whose World War Two-era work for the Nazi regime was more-or-less overlooked when he came to America post-war; the U.S. needed all the skills that this brilliant rocket scientist could bring to bear) and his engineers created a behemoth that could generate incredible brute force. The Saturn contained the largest single engine ever built, known as the F-1, with a thrust rating of 1.5 million pounds. Five F-1s together on the first stage created more than 7.5 million pounds of thrust, as each engine burned almost one million pounds of kerosene and liquid oxygen in less than three minutes. All of this power was necessary to launch the Saturn V which, when fully fueled and carrying maximum payload, weighed 6.5 million pounds. After liftoff, when the first stage fell away, the rocket became five million pounds lighter. The second and third stages brought the payload into orbit while burning liquid hydrogen and oxygen. The Saturn V proved itself time and again to be an engineering wonder.

The string of unmanned missions continued with Apollo 5 in January 1968. A Type-B mission launched by a Saturn 1B rocket, Apollo 5 marked the first tryout of the lunar module. There were successful checks on the ascent and descent engines, as well as a simulated landing abort, known by NASA engineers as a "fire-in-the-hole" test. One more unmanned mission, Apollo 6, originated in April. This marked confirmation of the Saturn V's ability to effectively complete translunar injection, a propulsive maneuver intended to put the spacecraft on the proper trajectory to the Moon. Despite some vibrations in the rocket engines and minor problems which would be swiftly corrected, NASA was now on track to initiate the first manned Apollo voyage.

Frank Borman had been designated the commander of Apollo 9, the third of four manned missions in the series. Apollo 9 would be fairly simple, running in early 1969, consisting of an Earth orbit and a series of tests, then a return trip home. In August of 1968, Borman and his two crewmates, Jim Lovell and Bill Anders, were knee-deep in the effort to make the command module the most advanced, safest spacecraft in the world. In the midst of the work, Borman received another urgent call from Deke Slayton. Borman said, "Deke, I'm in the middle of a big test here." Slayton insisted, "Frank, I need you back in Houston." Talk to me now," begged Borman, sadly remembering the last time he had been called to meet with Slayton after Apollo 1. "No, I can't talk over the phone. It's gotta be in person. Grab an airplane and get to Houston. On the double."

When Borman arrived, Slayton reported, "We just got word from the CIA that the Russians are planning a lunar fly-by before the end of the year. We want to change Apollo 8 from an Earth orbital to a lunar orbital flight. A lot has to come together. And Apollo 7 has to be perfect. But if it happens, Frank, do you want to go to the

Moon?" This mission would need to come together in just four months. There were serious doubts that the lunar module would be ready. Only a rapid and monumental effort could possibly succeed. Borman knew all this, and would have been fully justified in asking to think it over, but Slayton needed an answer now.

Author Robert Kurson explained the gravity of the moment: "Borman understood the urgency. If the Soviet Union sent men to the Moon first – even if those men didn't land – it would score a major victory in the Space Race and deal a devastating blow in the Cold War between the United States and the Soviet Union. The mission Slayton was proposing would be exquisitely dangerous. But it also had the power to change history. Now, suddenly, it all depended on the decision of Borman and his crew." Of course, the newly-minted men of Apollo 8 would be up to the challenge.

Throughout the entire journey, from Apollo 1 to Apollo 8 and beyond, the hundreds of thousands of people who contributed to NASA's epic quest demonstrated the two critical leadership dimensions of self-knowledge and learning, as well as energy and passion. Leadership happens at every level within an organization. Only by learning from past mistakes, open-minded experimentation, and gathering reams of new information could the team achieve the technical mastery required to go to the Moon. And only with an energetic, all-hands-on-deck work ethic, coupled with a passionate desire to overcome all obstacles, could the proposed Apollo 8 moon orbit be achieved in a mere 16 weeks. At every level, the team rolled up its collective sleeves and got down to business.

First things first: as Slayton had emphatically stated, Apollo 7 needed to be flawless. Walt Cunningham was a former Marine fighter pilot with a doctorate in physics. He was the lunar module pilot who, along with fellow astronauts Wally Schirra (mission commander) and Donn Eisele (command module pilot), would ride Apollo 7 into orbit in October 1968. As quoted in the publication *History of NASA: The Fascinating Story of the Iconic American Space Agency*, Cunningham summarized the importance and objectives of the mission: "Apollo 7 was considered – at the time – to be a very ambitious effort to make up for lost time. It was planned for 11 days to test all of the propulsion and all of the spacecraft systems, all of the docking, all of the rendezvous maneuvers, ground systems... you name it, it was tested." The flight was indeed close to faultless, circling the Earth 163 times. Cunningham summarized,

"To this day Apollo 7 is one of the most ambitious and most successful test flights of one of the first new flying machines ever. The spacecraft was near perfect. It was a wonderful accomplishment."

The crew of Apollo 8, Air Force Colonel Frank Borman (mission commander), Navy Captain James Lovell (command module pilot), and Air Force Major William Anders (lunar module pilot), took off atop a Saturn V rocket from Launchpad 39A at Kennedy Space Center at 7:50 am EST on December 21, 1968. The spacecraft orbited Earth one-and-one-half times, then the third stage booster began a four-minute burn to achieve translunar injection, thus pointing the craft's trajectory toward the Moon. Over the next several hours, the astronauts experienced something unique that no human had ever before encountered - they saw the Earth as a whole planet. And as they rocketed to the Moon, the home planet became eerily smaller and smaller in their field of vision.

The Apollo 8 mission was not without its tense moments. After 18 hours of flight time, Borman became ill with vomiting and diarrhea (as if there were not enough issues to deal with in the confined capsule). He got some sleep and said that he felt better, but Mission Control needed to be notified. In the spirit of decorum and not wanting to alert the public to the commander's gastrointestinal difficulties, the team used a private communication channel to report the situation. A flight surgeon consulted with Borman, and NASA officials ruled that the mission could continue and not be aborted. On the return flight, Lovell inadvertently erased computer memory. As a result, there occurred an unintentional thruster firing which caused a misalignment of the spacecraft. Lovell recovered nicely, manually calculating and entering the correct navigational information into the system, averting a potential disaster.

Apollo 8 made history over the seven-day duration of the journey by scoring a significant number of firsts. No manned mission had ever left Earth's orbit, orbited the Moon, and safely returned home. The crew was the first to go beyond a low orbit, and as they did, they saw the Earth in its magnificent entirety. They viewed the dark side of the Moon, and were out of contact with Mission Control. The men completed 10 Moon orbits, and precisely initiated the required engine burn on the dark side of the Moon to position the spacecraft for the return home. They were the first to leave the gravitational pull of another celestial body, the Moon, and then re-enter the gravitational well of the Earth. In an incredibly tumultuous year for America, which included war in Vietnam, political assassinations, and horrific domestic unrest, Apollo 8 represented a poignant reminder of what humanity is capable of at its best.

One of Apollo 8's main tasks was to conduct reconnaissance and take photos of the Moon's surface for the benefit of future missions. During the first three Moon orbits, the nose and windows of the craft were therefore pointed downward. On Christmas Eve, as they emerged from the fourth orbit, Borman reoriented the spacecraft toward the horizon for a navigational fix. Soon, a gorgeous blue-and-white object came into view. "Oh my God!" exclaimed Anders. "Look at that picture over there! Here's the Earth coming up. Wow is that pretty!" Anders scrambled to swap out his black-and-white camera film for color. He adjusted his exposure and quickly snapped multiple shots of the unforgettable scene, never before directly witnessed by human eyes. The best of the resulting images, later called *Earthrise,* became one of the most iconic photographs of all time (an abstract version of it graces the cover of this book), and an ongoing inspiration for the environmental movement.

Borman thought the sight of the Earth suspended in space the most beautiful he had ever seen. Lovell marveled at the smallness and fragility of the Earth, yet that it was home to 3.5 billion people, all of whom wanted the same simple things: health, prosperity, family, and a chance to live out their lives in peace and to the fullest. Anders reflected on the terrible year that had been 1968. But despite it all, when seeing the Earth from that vantage point, one could not help but conclude that, in the end, the only thing we have in the vast emptiness of the universe is each other. He said, "We came all this way to explore the Moon, and the most important thing is that we discovered the Earth."

Later on Christmas Eve, at 8:30 pm Houston time, television networks across America and the world interrupted normal programming. Within minutes, a fuzzy picture appeared. Frank Borman announced, "This is Apollo 8, coming to you live from the Moon." The crew proceeded to explain to viewers the varied activities they had engaged in, and their impressions of all that they had seen. Lovell spoke for the three of them when he said, "The vase loneliness up here of the Moon is awe-inspiring, and it makes you realize just what you have back there on Earth. The Earth from here is a grand oasis in the big vastness of space."

The crew continued to excitedly describe all that they were seeing, until they approached Apollo 11's future landing site at the Sea of Tranquility. Television time was nearly over. The astronauts briefly went silent. Finally Anders said, "We are now approaching lunar sunrise, and for all the people back on Earth, the crew of Apollo 8 has a message that we would like to send to you." He continued, "In the beginning, God created the heaven and the earth. And the earth was without form, and void, and darkness was upon the face of the deep." He was reading from King James and the Book of Genesis. "And the spirit of God moved upon the face of the waters. And God said, Let there be light: and there was light. And God saw the light, that it was good: and God divided the light from the darkness." Lovell continued: "And God called the light Day, and the darkness he called Night. And the evening and the morning were the first day. And God said, Let there be a firmament in the midst of the waters, and let it divide the waters from the waters. And God made the firmament, and divided the waters which were under the firmament from the waters which were above the firmament: and it was so. And God called the firmament Heaven. And the evening and the morning were the second day." Borman finished the passage: "And God said, Let the waters under the heaven be gathered together unto one place, and let the dry land appear: and it was so. And God called the dry land Earth; and the gathering together of the waters called he Seas: and God saw that it was good." There was a pause. Borman signed off by saying, "And from the crew of Apollo 8, we close with good night, good luck, a Merry Christmas, and God bless all of you – all of you on the good Earth."

The scientists and engineers in Mission Control were quiet and still. Within minutes, there was scarcely a dry eye in the house. The legendary Walter Cronkite, in his studio at CBS, stifled back tears as he closed off the broadcast. Television screens everywhere went dark. It is said that people the world over then went outside, looked up and scanned the heavens, hoping for a glimpse of - or given that impossibility - at least some spiritual connection with the three brave astronauts who had just deeply touched their hearts, from all the long way to the Moon, back to Mother Earth.

Anyone who stops learning is old, whether at twenty or eighty. Anyone who keeps learning stays young.

HENRY FORD

CHAPTER THREE

CASE STUDIES: SELF-KNOWLEDGE & LEARNING

"Are there contradictions? Let's start very explicitly with the fact that the Ford Foundation is a product of capitalism. Henry Ford never imagined that a Black gay man would be president of this foundation, but that's what's great about American philanthropy, that it continues to evolve." Darren Walker was named president of the Ford Foundation in 2013. He represents the very embodiment of the principle of self-knowledge and lifelong learning. He has used his education and expertise in working tirelessly to change the way we think about economic inequality and social justice in America. His incredible journey in the worlds of law, business and philanthropy – difficult though it has been at many points along the way – serves as a model for us all.

The Ford Foundation was established in 1936 with a $25,000 gift by Edsel Ford, son of the great automotive industrialist (and infamous bigot) Henry Ford. Edsel served as the first president. The founding charter identified "scientific, educational, and charitable purposes, all for the public welfare" as targeted areas for giving. By the mid-1940s, the foundation was the largest philanthropy in the world. Under the leadership of Edsel's son, Henry Ford II, a study group made suggestions as to how the foundation should best direct its prolific giving. The board of trustees approved the recommendations in 1949. Going forward, the foundation would focus on an international effort to advance human welfare by reducing poverty and promoting education, democratic values and peace. The foundation established headquarters in New York City in 1953. Currently, in 2022, according to the official website, "The foundation is an independent organization, led by a distinguished board of trustees whose 16 members hail from four continents and bring leadership and expertise in a wide range of disciplines. Today we are stewards of a $14 billion endowment, making $500 million in grants around the world every year. Led by Darren Walker, our 10th president, we remain committed to our enduring mission—and to our legacy of bold, creative support for social change."

Darren Walker is the son of a single mother who supported him by working as a nurse's aide. He grew up poor in Louisiana and East Texas. He is entirely a product of the public school system. The young boy's future changed dramatically and for the better when, in 1965, he was recruited to become a member of the first preschool class of Head Start, a newly minted federal initiative designed to reduce poverty. In an interview with the CBS news program *60 Minutes* in April 2021, Walker reflected: "I knew I was a lucky child. I felt that my country was cheering me on." In that same program Walker's mother, Beulah Spencer, said, "I knew the Lord had something good in store for Darren." She emphasized, "Education, education, education." She used part of her limited income to purchase the entire set of Encyclopedia Britannica for Darren and his sister, one volume at a time. Walker further advanced his education, earning B.A., B.S. and J.D. degrees from the University of Texas-Austin. He later characterized his special opportunity as a "mobility escalator," funded with public dollars that, he fears, is probably no longer available to people like he was, seeking to escape poverty. Walker began his professional career in New York City, in 1986, as an associate in the law firm Cleary Gottlieb Steen & Hamilton, moving on after a couple of years to a seven-year stint as a bond trader at the Union Bank of Switzerland.

At the University of Texas, Walker had been known as a charismatic presence, an academic star who was also warm, kind, and adept at bringing all kinds of people together. He continued to display those traits as his career progressed. He volunteered at the Children's Storefront School in Harlem. He worked to establish an extensive network of power players, community leaders and regular citizens, creating productive alliances everywhere he went through the force of his engaging personality. In 1992, Walker met an art dealer named David Beitzel, and they became a couple (Beitzel died of heart failure in 2019 – Walker was quoted in a *New York Times* special publication called *Leadership*, saying, "David was a better human being than me.") In the late 1990s, Walker became the chief operating officer of the Abyssinian Development Corporation, a non-profit group that marshalled public and private funds to restore dilapidated buildings in Harlem. The corporation then used its profits to acquire and restore additional buildings. Walker went on to join the Rockefeller Foundation and then the Ford Foundation, eventually ascending to the top job.

From the very start, Darren Walker's vision and primary focus centered on addressing inequality; this, however, was a task easier said than done. He was deeply familiar with the traditional view of philanthropy, as originally articulated by the industrialist Andrew Carnegie in an 1889 article entitled "The Gospel of Wealth." Carnegie's belief was that inequality was a given, a reflection of the natural order of the world. But he also argued that those who had been fortunate enough to accumulate great wealth had a moral obligation to give back. Carnegie declared, "This, then, is held to be the duty of the man of wealth. To consider all surplus revenues which come to him simply as trust funds, which he is called upon to administer... in the manner which, in his judgment, is best calculated to produce the most beneficial results for the community." Walker was convinced that this approach was outdated and no longer worked.

Walker also understood the conundrum that high-dollar philanthropy is only made possible by the very inequality he wanted to tackle. The system perpetuates inequality by increasing the influence of wealthy elites, who are really not accountable to anyone in their giving. Affluent donors and foundations receive generous tax breaks, which are in effect subsidized by the rest of us, to the tune of - according to one estimate - $50 billion annually.

Walker was perplexed at the challenges and contradictions. The lack of diversity in the world of philanthropy troubled him. As another example, the Ford Foundation provided funding for Native people who endeavored to recover sacred land from developers; yet, the foundation also invested in companies that desecrated that very same land through mining and logging. In his 2019 book, *From Generosity to Justice: A New Gospel of Wealth*, Walker asks the question: "How can we move our work along the continuum from generosity to justice?" He has spent years on a learning journey, contemplating that question, and working toward an answer.

At Ford, Walker has implemented changes, some subtle, some significant. He substantially downsized the dimensions of his own office, moving into a smaller space with windows so everyone could see him. He sold the foundation's entire existing art collection, 400 works, all but one by white men, and then purchased more than 300 new works, many of them by women and people of color. He integrated Ford's arts and social justice programs, providing less funding for well-established institutions like the Lincoln Center, and more for smaller, less well-known arts organizations in places such as Harlem.

Today, the foundation proudly and simply declares its mission as "Challenging Inequality." Walker fully realizes that it is not in human nature to give up privilege, especially if there is a perception that it has been hard earned. He also readily admits he is himself a privileged insider. He acknowledges that in his lifetime, he has gone from the bottom one percent of society to – with his salary of close to one million dollars per year – the top one percent. But, he says, "At the end of the day, we elites need to understand that while we may be benefiting from this inequality, ultimately we are undoing the very fabric of America. We are going to have to give up some of our privilege if we want to survive."

In a June 2020 *New York Times* Op Ed piece entitled, "Are You Willing to Give up Your Privilege?" Walker is very clear about the enormity of what is at stake: "This is the most pressing work of our time, and it will be difficult. Our present is deeply rooted in historical inequalities that must methodically be rectified. But difficulty is not an excuse to allow American capitalism to grow more distorted, corrupt and unjust. It does not relieve us of our duty to strengthen and improve a system that, if rebalanced, could once again make America a beacon for upward mobility. Without hope, American dreams deferred or denied will continue, as the poet Langston Hughes wrote, to explode. With hope, and through it, we can reimagine the dream and invite many millions more to share in its promise."

The Ford Foundation identifies five underlying drivers of inequality: entrenched cultural narratives; failure to invest in and protect public goods; unfair rules of the economy; unequal access to government; and, persistent prejudice and discrimination. Accordingly, the specific focus for giving is in the following areas: cities and states; civic engagement and government; creativity and free expression; the future of work(ers); gender, racial and ethnic justice; natural resources and climate change; and, technology and society.

Through it all, Darren Walker has been the driving force. He is desperately curious, always seeking new information. Ford's website chronicles the many achievements of a true Renaissance Man: "Darren co-chairs New York City's Mayoral Advisory Commission on City Art, Monuments, and Markers, and has served on the Independent Commission on New York City Criminal Justice and Incarceration Reform and the UN International Labour Organization Global Commission on the Future of Work. He co-founded both the US Impact Investing Alliance and the Presidents' Council on Disability Inclusion in Philanthropy. He serves on many boards, including Lincoln Center for the Performing Arts, the National Gallery of Art, Carnegie Hall, the High Line, the Committee to Protect Journalists, and the Smithsonian National Museum of African American History & Culture. In the summer of 2020, he was appointed to the boards of Square and Ralph Lauren. He is a member of the Council on Foreign Relations, the American Academy of Arts and Sciences and is the recipient of 16 honorary degrees and university awards, including Harvard University's W.E.B. Du Bois Medal."

In his book, Walker neatly sums up the key questions that leaders must continually address in the pursuit of knowledge, progress and change: "As leaders, we must ask ourselves: *What do we* not *know about? What biases do we bring to the table? What ignorance do we harbor? And whom must we talk to, where must we go, and what must we do to learn more about the areas and experiences where we may lack expertise?*" Philanthropy historian Ben Soskis of the Urban Institute says of Walker, "It's hard to overemphasize how little inequality had been a philanthropic concern over the last half-century. He took on a huge challenge. There's been no figure with greater influence in the sector than Darren Walker."

Can an old dog learn new tricks? Frequently no; sometimes, emphatically, yes. In 2021, Bruce Arians, head coach of the Tampa Bay Buccaneers turned 69 years old; he is the third-oldest head coach in the National Football League (NFL). His counterpart Andy Reid, head coach of the Kansas City Chiefs, at 63, is the sixth-oldest coach in the league. In January 2021, these two veteran leaders and their teams met in a much-anticipated Super Bowl contest. Both teams reflected and embodied their respective coaches' philosophy that in football, as in business and life, one must be forever learning and adapting to new, changing circumstances in order to reach the mountaintop.

By his own count, Bruce Arians has been fired and/or moved on from one coaching position to another 11 times. At one point early in his career, he and his young family lived in six different cities in 15 years. He was an assistant at multiple colleges and finally became a head coach at Temple University, from 1983-1988. He worked himself to sickness in that job. In an ESPN special, *A Football Life*, Arians admitted, "I did not know how to delegate." He suffered from excruciating migraine headaches. "I got fired, and I've never had a migraine since" (we can safely assume that he also learned how to delegate.)

Arians, known as "BA" to his players, went on to serve as a longtime NFL offensive assistant, who developed a reputation as a "quarterback whisperer." He got his first NFL head coaching job in 2012 when he stepped in on an interim basis for the Indianapolis Colts, in place of Chuck Pagano, who was battling leukemia. Arians won the AP NFL Coach of the Year Award in leading a team that had gone 2-14 the previous season to a 9-3 record and the playoffs. He was hired by the Arizona Cardinals the next year. Over five seasons, he was named Coach of the Year again (2014) and led the Cardinals to the postseason twice, a division title, and the 2015 NFC Championship Game. Arians retired in 2017, but was lured back into the game he loves in 2019 to coach the Tampa Bay Buccaneers. He took that team to the Super Bowl in his second season. Over an nine-year span, Arians has amassed a record of 86-51-1.

Andy Reid is also a football lifer. He began his career in the NFL as an offensive assistant with the Green Bay Packers in 1992. Over seven seasons he gained valuable experience and realized the thrill of winning a Super Bowl, in 1997. He was named head coach of the Philadelphia Eagles in 1999. The team enjoyed great consistency and success with nine postseason appearances, six division titles, five NFC Championship Game appearances (four in a row from 2001-2004), but only one Super Bowl, a heartbreaking loss to the New England Patriots in 2004. Reid gained a reputation for tremendous regular season results, but an inability to win the big game. The Eagles fired him in 2012 after two losing seasons. The Chiefs hired Reid in 2013, and have achieved eight playoff appearances under his leadership. They finally won the elusive prize, Super Bowl LIV, in 2020. In 2021, they hoped to become one of only eight teams (the Pittsburgh Steelers did it twice) to win consecutive Super Bowls. Reid's career record is 252-151-1.

The late, great coach Bum Philips is supposed to have said, "There's two kinds of coaches, them that's fired and them that's gonna be fired." In his book, *The Q Factor: The Elusive Search for the Next Great NFL Quarterback,* former Super Bowl-winning head coach Brian Billick summarizes why this aphorism is true, over time, for the vast majority of NFL head coaches: "If... coaches lose their jobs when their old ways of coaching sputter, why don't they change, or try to change, before they get the pink slip? Some are stubborn. *I'm smart. I know what I'm doing. Look at my record.* Some are too old. *I've always done it this way. I'm not chasing some fad.* And some don't know how. *Huh?*"

In a fascinating 2018 study produced by the *Harvard Business Review* for its *Working Knowledge* publication, three academic scholars address parallels between job performance and tenure in business and the NFL. They ask the question, "Why did coaches succeed or fail in a league that some scholars have referred to as a natural laboratory for studying performance? When and why did previously successful coaches lose their powers?" In addition, they "... examined this link between tenure and job performance among business managers, finding that some are able to maintain job performance by adapting and staying relevant, while others do not; they see their job performance decline over time, ultimately leading to their dismissal."

The authors used NFL data from 2000-2015 to study coaching tenure and effectiveness. What they found is that the very best coaches (defined as those who have won Super Bowls and/or stayed with the same team for 10 seasons or more) share a series of skills and attributes: these leaders are highly adaptable to change in the industry, and they further adapt based on team strengths and weaknesses; they leverage competitive resources and are skilled at making changes at the margins; they communicate well and establish strong relationships with all key stakeholders; they outsource tasks which they are not themselves good at; finally, they stay curious and learn from others, including those outside the organization. While Andy Reid and Bruce Arians have demonstrated all of these capabilities over the course of their long careers, it is in the final realm, around curiosity and learning, where they have both truly excelled.

In a January 2020 article from the *Ringer Newsletter* entitled, "Andy Reid's Beautiful Mind," Chief's receivers' coach Greg Lewis says, "He studies like no other coach I've ever been around. He studies college games, high school games, CFL games, *European* games. He'll go look at stuff from 1910. He knows everything. He has a beautiful mind. He is able to compartmentalize everything then bring it out at the right moment. 'Oh, this is something I saw on film from 70 years ago.' ....He is so open to adapting and adjusting the nuances of the offense. He has never been stuck on what he did before." And then, most importantly, "He's able to put it in terms everyone understands, and that's special."

Reid is a disciple of the West Coast offensive scheme, which he learned from a master, Mike Holmgren, during his tenure in Green Bay. The West Coast offense, originally developed by legendary San Francisco 49ers coach Bill Walsh, relies on short, horizontal passing routes that get the ball quickly into the hands of skilled playmakers in the open field. Football is a sport that develops over time not based on massive changes, but on incremental, nuanced modifications to existing ideas. Reid has not been a great inventor, but rather a master at tweaking his offenses (i.e., "making changes at the margin") season by season.

Minneapolis Star Tribune sports reporter Mark Craig had an opportunity to interview Reid. In a piece just prior to the 2021 Super Bowl, Craig said, "Through it all, Reid's personality has never changed. Players say they don't play 'for' Reid but rather 'with' him... 'I try to treat people the way I would want to be treated,' Reid said. 'You don't have to yell and scream at me to get me to do something better. I know I just would turn that person off and probably not listen to anything they said. I look at myself as a teacher of men.'" Chiefs' defensive coach Brendan Daly, who used to compete with Reid as a Patriots assistant, observed, "At one point in time, I used to think of Coach Reid as one of the bare-bones offensive coaches. It has been fascinating to see him, over the years, as offenses change, as players change. Competing against him ... I was so impressed by how incredibly open-minded he was to new concepts, to new ideas. Formations, plays – his ability to incorporate so many new things into his offense but holding the same characteristics he's had his entire career."

"I live life and call plays the same way," philosophizes Bruce Arians. "No risk it, no biscuit... you can't live scared." Like Andy Reid, Arians has always had a different take on the game of football from the typical coach. He eschews the grueling hours that most coaches consider mandatory and the price of admission to the profession. "When I hear of guys in their office till all hours, I wonder what the hell they're doing there. This game ain't that hard." He tells his assistants, "The work will always be there, but your kids won't… If you miss a recital, piano, dance, whatever, a football game, a basketball game, I'll fire you." And he means it. He coached for two years under the legendary Paul "Bear" Bryant at Alabama (he has kept a portrait of Bryant in his office for 30 years since then.) Bryant told him that when it comes to his players, "Coach 'em hard and hug 'em later." In a sport where some coaches consider their players to be no more than fungible parts of the machine, who can be used and discarded as necessary, Arians is different. Cardinals All-Pro receiver Larry Fitzgerald says that Arians is "… constantly challenging you… but nobody cares more about you than Coach." The ESPN special captured Arians at the front of the room in a team meeting. He preaches, "If your football sucks, I'm gonna tell you that your football sucks. But I love you as a guy." His players love him right back.

Brian Billick summarizes the practical meaning of Arians' "no risk it, no biscuit" philosophy: "Play aggressively; give the quarterback two plays on every snap; create trust between quarterback and coach and team. Break down the coach-player wall, relate as peers, and have a drink – [Arians] says he learned his most important lessons in human nature while bartending." Arians is known as an especially talented teacher of quarterbacks; Peyton Manning, among many others, perfected his craft under Arians' tutelage. One of those quarterbacks, Carson Palmer, commented on Arians as an innovator: "Everyone in the league is copy-catting, and you see what he is doing and it's totally different."

One key area in which the Buccaneers have been different than the rest of the league is diversity. The NFL has a quite abysmal record when it comes to hiring general managers and coaches, especially head coaches, of color. This despite the reams of data over many years demonstrating that diverse teams and coaching staffs have more success than those that are not diverse. Arians employs Black coaches in all four primary spots: Byron Leftwich is his offensive coordinator; Todd Bowles runs the defense; Keith Armstrong coordinates special teams; and Harold Godwin is the assistant head coach and running game coordinator. In addition, the Bucs are the only team in the league with two women as full-time coaches: Lori Locust is assistant defensive line coach and Maral Javadifar is the assistant strength and conditioning coach. In February 2021, after the Super Bowl, ESPN football analyst Ryan Clark tweeted, "Thank you Bruce Arians for showing the world that all 3 of your coordinators can be black, your assistant head coach can be black, you can have two full-time women coaches, and be the best team in the world. BA you're a trailblazer. Leadership doesn't have a look."

Arians and his geriatric 43-year-old quarterback Tom Brady, the GOAT (Greatest of All Time), soundly defeated Andy Reid and his 25-year-old phenom of a quarterback, Patrick Mahomes, in the 55th Super Bowl. Despite the lopsided 31-9 score, both coaches deserve high credit for having come so far and done so well in their NFL journeys. As sportswriter Mark Craig says, "Both men are old-school yet open-minded and up to date as cutting edge offensive minds. They're in control but not controlling. Patient, yet aggressive. Teachers, not screamers. Leaders who are comfortable in their own wrinkled skin." Andy Reid and Bruce Arians prove that even those of us with gray hair and wrinkled skin can occasionally learn a new trick; those who fail to do so have been known to go by the wayside.

The consciousness-raising, the advocacy, the passion, the youth of your movement is so critical.

HILLARY CLINTON

CHAPTER FOUR

CASE STUDIES: ENERGY & PASSION

The World Economic Forum is an annual gathering in Davos, Switzerland, of movers and shakers in politics, business, science, academe, and entertainment. During a luncheon at the January 2019 meeting, a 16-year-old Swedish climate activist named Greta Thunberg – who gained fame as the organizer of a school strike for climate action outside of the Swedish Parliament building – told the gathered elite of global thought and leadership: "I don't want your hope... I want you to panic... I want you to act as you would in a crisis. I want you to act as if the house is on fire, because it is."

Greta Thunberg is the quintessential representative of a worldwide youth movement that is, with respect to climate change (and other issues as well, such as social justice and economic inequality), mad as hell and not going to take it anymore. The energy and passion of these young people, numbering in the millions, especially around climate change, has become a force to be reckoned with. Business leaders need to pay attention.

Former President Donald Trump spent the four years of his administration characterizing climate change as a "very expensive hoax," at one point even blaming it on the Chinese. He and his government actively worked to undo much of the progress that had been made on this critical issue. At the World Economic Forum, Thunberg found it a bit surreal when she was cast by the media as the antithesis to Trump. Thunberg was named *Time* magazine's person of the year in 2019, at which time Trump suggested on Twitter that she work on her "anger management problem" and "go to an old-fashioned movie with a friend." "Chill Greta, chill!" Thunberg bided her time until, almost a year later, as Trump raged about voter fraud in the 2020 elections, she tweeted, "Donald must work on his Anger Management problem, then go to a good old-fashioned movie with a friend! Chill Donald, Chill!" Indeed, Thunberg has no hesitation about speaking truth to – or thumbing her nose at - power.

On Earth Day, April 22, 2021, a BBC documentary about Thunberg called, *A Year to Change the World*, premiered on PBS. In it, she took a year off of school (which process was unfortunately derailed and delayed by the pandemic) to visit various sites heavily impacted by climate change. Among other places, she toured melting glaciers in the Canadian Rockies, a Polish coal mine, and a town in California ravaged by wildfires. The documentary summarizes her life and improbable rise to prominence and power. She is on the autism spectrum, which has lent a unique lucidity and focused resolve to her activism. She said, "I don't follow social codes. Everyone else seems to be playing a role, just going on like before. And I, who am autistic, I don't play this social game." She reflects on the pandemic and laments the lack of urgency concerning her own cause: "If we humans would actually start treating the climate crisis like a crisis, we could really change things." She does not mince words and refuses to engage in false optimism; as a result, her energy and passion are sometimes misunderstood. In an April 2021 interview in the *New Yorker*, she said, "People seem to think I am depressed, or angry, or worried, but that's not true." Like countless other young people the world over, she is happy to champion what she sees as the existential challenge of our time. "It was like I got meaning in my life."

The Planet Earth is roughly 4.5 billion years old. Earth's geology and climate have been ever-changing, continually and sometimes drastically, for eons. Continents have mashed together and torn apart. My home state, the northern tundra called Minnesota, apparently once sat near the equator. Over time, the Earth has cycled between ice ages that covered much of the planet in massive sheets of ice, and warmer interglacial periods such as the one we live in presently. The frigid polar regions have at various points in Earth's past been green, lush and tropical. And so, undoubtedly, massive changes have always happened in the natural course of the life of the Earth.

What is different today regarding climate is the pace and magnitude of the changes. Since the Industrial Revolution, as a result of the burning of fossil fuels by humans and the subsequent release of carbon into the atmosphere, carbon dioxide concentrations have increased by almost 50 percent. Today, the level of carbon in the atmosphere is at 420 parts per million, which is the highest reading in three million years. The concentration of carbon is also increasing at approximately 100 times the rate as it did when the last ice age ended. Global warming exacerbates droughts and increases the intensity of rain and flooding. The polar icecaps are melting with alarming rapidity, resulting in rising waters. The oceans absorb more than 90 percent of the carbon that is emitted into the atmosphere, and so oceans are warming too. The result is increasing acidity, loss of habitat, and the death of reefs. There is strong evidence that global warming, while it may not increase the frequency of hurricanes, makes them longer lasting and more violent. Wildfires have many causes too, but climate change increases their likelihood, size and fury by heating and drying forests, creating tinderbox conditions.

According to scientists at NASA's Goddard Institute for Space Studies (GISS) in New York, Earth's global average surface temperature in 2020 tied with 2016 as the warmest year on record. Gavin Schmidt, Director of GISS, reported, "The last seven years have been the warmest seven years on record, typifying the ongoing and dramatic warming trend. Whether one year is a record or not is not really that important – the important things are long-term trends. With these trends, and as the human impact on the climate increases, we have to expect that records will continue to be broken."

Climatologists agree that climate science is complex, and that to make accurate predictions about exactly what will transpire in the future is difficult. But they also agree, with an astounding level of consensus that is unusual in the scientific community, about what is happening to the Earth. Numerous studies indicate that more than 90 percent of climate researchers concur that global warming is real, that it is upon us, and that it is mostly man-made. Scientists also urge that humanity must take immediate and dramatic action in order to prevent the worst long-term outcomes from climate change.

For many people, such dire facts cause a sense of despair and hopelessness. Is there any chance that we can possibly overcome this problem which so dramatically affects us all, whether we like it or not? Young people around the world – who have inherited the mess that previous generations have left to them - are determined to never give up and fight for a better future.

In the United States, for example, a group of teenagers formed an organization called Zero Hour, which is described as "an environmentally focused, creatively minded and technologically savvy nationwide coalition." The mission of Zero Hour is "to center the voices of diverse youth in the conversation around climate and environmental justice." The group commenced their campaign with a protest march in July 2018 at the National Mall in Washington D.C., conducted in concert with sister demonstrations across the nation. Zero Hour's leadership team met with nearly 40 federal lawmakers to explain their platform. Their objective is to inspire other young people to step up, get organized, and demand radical action on climate change. Zero Hour has received financial support and sponsorship offers from dozens of established environmental and advocacy groups. Jamie Margolin, 16 years old at the time, had the original idea for Zero Hour. As the movement grew in strength and momentum she said, "We flipped the scenario as the underdog. We've proven ourselves. We are on the verge of something amazing. We're going to change history." She may be right.

In April 2021, at the commencement of a two-day virtual climate summit, President Joe Biden announced America's moonshot goal to cut U.S. climate warming emissions in half by 2030. The tide is moving inexorably in a positive direction, and business leaders who fail to take notice do so at their peril. Larry Fink is the CEO of BlackRock, the world's largest asset manager, with more than $9 trillion under management. In an early 2021 letter to CEOs, Fink warned: "There is no company whose business model won't be profoundly affected by the transition to a net zero economy – one that emits no more carbon dioxide than it removes from the atmosphere by 2050, the scientifically-established threshold necessary to keep global warming well below 2°C. As the transition accelerates, companies with a well-articulated long-term strategy, and a clear plan to address the transition to net zero, will distinguish themselves with their stakeholders – with customers, policymakers, employees and shareholders – by inspiring confidence that they can navigate this global transformation. But companies that are not quickly preparing themselves will see their businesses and valuations suffer, as these same stakeholders lose confidence that those companies can adapt their business models to the dramatic changes that are coming."

It seems that more and more, companies and their investors can indeed do well by doing good. Environmental, social and governance (ESG) funds invest their assets in companies that either avoid harm or actively do social good – with a special focus on sustainability. In 2020, with the pandemic, social unrest, and climate disasters abounding, net new investment flowed into ESG funds to the tune of more than $51 billion. Those investors generally did well: the median ESG fund outperformed traditional funds by four percent. A 2020 survey of 375 global executives by law firm Herbert Smith Freehills LLP found that 80 percent of companies expect an increase in employee activism, with climate concerns as a top priority. In an April 2021 editorial in the *Wall Street Journal*, columnist Gerald F. Seib reported, "That expectation of corporate stand-taking is especially high among younger Americans. So businesses are feeling the pressure from both younger customers and their own employees to take stands. Companies hoping to recruit young, tech-savvy talent know that corporate culture and reputation now are part of the equation potential employees consider when deciding where to land."

To be sure, there are passionate people of all ages (myself included) who care deeply about our climate crisis. To address the problem, we must all do our part. But the immense power of energized, organized, mobilized youth to force seismic global change is real. Primatologist and conservationist Jane Goodall said in a *Time* magazine essay in early 2019, "My greatest reason for hope for our future is the passion of young people. When we listen to them and empower them, the next generation is desperate to protect nature... Today in some 80 countries, groups are taking action to heal the harms we have inflicted... The challenges we face are daunting, but nature is resilient, the human intellect incredible. So now, as our youth join forces to tackle problems we have created, let us give them the support they need and help them in their fight to save the natural world – on which we ourselves depend."

Eric Yuan is the founder and CEO of Zoom. He was born as Yuan Zheng in 1980, in Tai'an, China. In perhaps the most prominent example from his youth of the incredible energy and passion that he has displayed throughout his life, he was rejected for a U.S. visa a demoralizing eight times; and yet he persisted. In an interview with *Time* magazine in December 2020, he reflected on the experience: "I was just so frustrated. But I was going to keep trying until they tell me, 'Don't come here anymore.'" Finally, he received his H-1 visa in 1997. Ten years later he realized his dream of becoming an American citizen. As of March 2021, he had a net worth of nearly $15 billion and is listed by *Forbes* magazine as among the wealthiest people in the world.

As a college student, Yuan studied math and science at Shandong University. He began dating the woman who later became his wife, but she attended college 10 hours away. Yuan fantasized about how wonderful it would be to see her face without having to spend half of a day traveling to be with her in person. He became tech-obsessed, and when he arrived in the U.S. he developed into a videoconferencing guru at WebEx, which was acquired by Cisco in 2007. Four years later Yuan left the company (taking a number of his talented WebEx teammates with him) to start his own videoconferencing platform, called Zoom, based in San Jose, California.

One of the most powerful factors in Zoom's success has been that, for the most part, and in 40-minute increments, it is free. The software came on the market in 2013, offering a basic package at no cost, but also with a number of paid tiers that provided different features and pricing depending on any given organization's needs. Zoom is cloud-based, simple to use, and does not require an account or an app. In addition to business networks, Zoom became prevalent in educational settings. Growth was steady and Zoom was identified in 2017 as a "unicorn", with a valuation of $1 billion. But Yuan's ambitions remained modest and he was not overly anxious to expand into consumer markets. The company went public in 2019 and generated considerable enthusiasm. In addition to high employee satisfaction scores, Zoom was a profitable company that carried no debt. Yuan was quoted in the *Time* feature: "In December [2019], our plans were the same as before: no big ideas, just keep innovating."

When the pandemic, social distancing, and sheltering in place became the sad new reality for the world in early 2020, Zoom experienced an unprecedented surge in global usage. People working from home, students and teachers forced into distance learning, and families and friends unable to gather in person, among many others, all looked to Zoom to help them connect. The number of daily participants in Zoom meetings rocketed from approximately 10 million in December 2019 to over 300 million in April 2020. In Q1 2020, Zoom's annualized meeting minutes increased by a factor of 20; revenues shot up 169 percent from the same quarter in 2019. The stock price tripled from pre-pandemic levels by the end of 2020. In addition to energy and passion, Yuan's response to Zoom's astronomical growth required adaptability and a bit of humility as well.

Not everything went smoothly. Zoom quickly ran into criticism concerning design problems, security lapses, and data sharing practices. In March 2020, New York's attorney general launched an investigation into Zoom's privacy and security policies, which in some cases had left users exposed to surveillance and harassment. In April, rather than fighting the charges, Yuan did the right thing, apologized profusely, and put a freeze on new innovation; he then committed to fixing the numerous issues that had been identified, as soon as possible. Among other steps, Zoom swiftly released a significant number of new safety measures, such as improved encryption and better transparency. These steps, executed nimbly, decisively, and with sincerity, won Yuan trust and praise from many former critics.

There were other problems as well, which are perhaps not as easy to solve. Users began to realize the phenomenon known as "Zoom fatigue." This very real condition amounts to much more than just a sore rear end from sitting in front of a screen all day. A 2021 study from Stanford University specifically identifies some of the other challenges associated with communicating via videoconference. As reported in an article entitled "Working online: Virtual insanity," from *The Economist*: "The first problem with video calls is that they force people to stare at their colleagues in close-up. Talk to someone on a laptop using the default configuration on Zoom and their face appears about as big as it would be if the two of you were standing 50c apart. At such proximity the brain is hard-wired to expect either a punch or a kiss." In addition, the endless eye contact that must be maintained in a video call is unnatural and makes people uncomfortable. Most of us can agree that it's just a little weird. An important part of human communication involves non-verbal cues, which are easy to pick up when we are face-to-face, but cannot be detected on a Zoom call. We nod more dramatically online. We talk louder than necessary. We don't see people fidget when we are boring them to tears. We experience delays in transmission that give conversations a herky-jerky quality. The result of all of this is not only exhaustion but greater difficulty in building the trust that only becomes possible by reading social cues in person.

Even Eric Yuan himself, in an interview with the *Wall Street Journal* in May 2021, acknowledged that after a day in which he had been on 19 Zoom calls (!), he too suffered from Zoom fatigue. But this and other issues aside, the positive outcomes from the online meeting revolution have been impressive. Simply put, Zoom and its competitors (Apple, Google and Microsoft, among others) in the videoconferencing arena have made remote work possible in the time of the pandemic. Countless employers no doubt feared that work from home would not be nearly as productive as the "butts in chairs in the office where I can see them" model that had been in place – and generally worked well, at least from management's point of view - for generations.

To the surprise of many, homebound employees are not idly streaming movies all day but are instead working hard. A September 2020 study by Harvard Business School looked at three million remote workers from 21,500 different companies. The research found that when work shifted online, people generally put in longer hours, managed a greater volume of email and, no shocker, they attended more meetings. Given these findings, it will be fascinating to see what employers do when society and our workplaces fully open up again. Some, like Goldman Sachs for example, will insist that everybody get back to the office. Others, such as Google, have told employees they can work from home permanently. A study by the research firm Gartner predicts that by 2024 only one quarter of business meetings will take place face-to-face. In all likelihood, most companies will try to keep employees happy and productive by establishing some reasonable middle ground that allows for both remote and in-person options.

On the world political front, Zoom has helped keep the wheels of foreign relations spinning. A May 2021 report in *The Economist* entitled "Hybrid diplomacy: The virtue of the virtual," says, "Virtual diplomacy is no joke. It has kept international relations ticking over during the past year, as travel became harder and face-to-face meetings often impossible. In the process, it has enlarged the diplomatic toolkit. Diplomats can make ample use of this in the post-pandemic future, too." Again, in some delicate or high-stakes situations, there simply is no substitute for in-person, sit-down discussions between international diplomats and political leaders. But, as *The Economist* reports, "It would be wrong to assume that diplomacy will simply return to business as usual... For one thing, virtual diplomacy has proved that it can be highly efficient.... Diplomacy will go hybrid. That could allow it to be more inclusive. The pandemic has intensified experiments in bringing a wider range of voices to conflict resolution.... In the 19th century the telegraph shrank the time needed to contact envoys. In the 20th century the jet plane shrank distance. Now digital platforms are supplanting physical presence. Used wisely, diplomacy will be the better for it."

Beyond the impacts on business and politics, there have been broader societal positives as well. In naming Eric Yuan its Businessperson of the Year for 2020, *Time* magazine said, "Yuan… found himself serving as the world's relationship liaison, social chair, principal, convention-center host, chief security officer and pallbearer." While professional sectors were the earliest adapters of Zoom technology, the impact on education has been significant as well. Yuan offered Zoom's platform to educators for free, and 125,000 K-12 schools around the country took him up on the offer. Online learning also has its disadvantages, but the alternative, a completely lost year or more of educational opportunity for a generation of students, is horrible to contemplate.

Perhaps most important, Zoom has allowed human beings to stay socially connected in a time of enormous isolation, loneliness and disconnectedness. *Time* describes how people adapted to Zoom: "They used it for birthday parties, family gatherings, workouts, company meetings, happy hours, blind dates… New York legalized Zoom marriages, to Yuan's delight…" The energy and passion that Yuan and his team have displayed not just in recent times, but over the past decade, has made it all possible. In an interview with Goldman Sachs in June 2020, Yuan described the journey: "Overall I think the experience has been totally unprecedented but the good news is that our team, we're working very hard on this opportunity to transform our business to become a bigger, stronger company. But what's more is that we're proud we can help the world give so many families an ability to stay connected. I personally do not think I have a single day where I was working on something else. Over the past now 10 years, every day, my team and myself have thought about that: how to make Zoom better, how to build a frictionless, collaborative experience, how to improve quality, how to support our customers well."

PART TWO

APOLLO 11

A weathered, sun-seared peach pit.

**MICHAEL COLLINS
DESCRIBING THE MOON IN HIS
AUTOBIOGRAPHY *CARRYING THE FIRE***

CHAPTER FIVE

APOLLO 11: ONE GIANT LEAP

"I'd be a liar or a fool if I said I had the best seat on Apollo 11," Michael Collins admitted to *Time* magazine in 2019, "But I can say absolutely, with total honesty, I was delighted to have the seat I had."

Collins died at a hospice facility in Naples, Florida on April 28, 2021, at the age of 90, of cancer. He is best remembered as the third guy, the astronaut who went all the way to the Moon in July 1969 but never got a chance to set foot on the objective. Instead, he flew the command module, *Columbia*, maintaining a steady orbit 60 miles above as Neil Armstrong and Buzz Aldrin became the first human beings to tread upon the lunar surface. Collins made it his mission, during the interval he spent aloft and by himself, to focus on the common purpose, make good decisions, and ensure that his comrades had a safe return ride to Earth. In so doing, he exemplified the extraordinary commitment of hundreds of thousands of talented, dedicated people to the lofty purpose, defiantly pronounced by JFK in 1961, of being first to reach the Moon. Collins also made sound decisions throughout the course of the mission, and was able to do so only as a result of countless good decisions made before, by engineers, designers, scientists, political leaders and others, up to his moment in the spotlight, all of which contributed to the legendary success of Apollo 11.

Collins was known as a thoughtful, reflective man, with a touch of the poet about him. His 1974 book, *Carrying the Fire*, is beautifully written. In it, he described his experience in the *Columbia* as he orbited to the dark side of the Moon and then back again: "I am alone now, truly alone, and absolutely isolated from any known life. If a count were taken, the score would be three billion plus two over on the other side of the Moon, and one plus God only knows what on this side. I like the feeling. Outside my window I can see the stars – and this is all. Where I know the Moon to be, there is simply a black void.... My windows suddenly flash full of sunlight as *Columbia* swings around into the dawn. The Moon appears quickly, dark, gray and craggy."

In a book written in 1990 about a hypothetical journey, called *Mission to Mars*, Collins attempted to capture the wonder and beauty of space travel: "I have been places and done things you simply would not believe. I feel like saying: I have dangled from a cord a hundred miles up; I have seen the earth eclipsed by the moon, and enjoyed it. I have seen the sun's true light, unfiltered by any planet's atmosphere. I have seen the ultimate black of infinity in a stillness undisturbed by any living thing. I do have this secret, this precious thing, that I will always carry with me."

Perhaps no single example in all of American history better demonstrates the leadership dimension called common purpose than the Apollo Moon landing. All of the men and women who worked on the project, both inside and outside of NASA, clearly understood the single compelling idea that unified them and drove the organization forward: we will put a man on the Moon before the 1960s are out. Some may not have liked the idea, or believed that the goal was even possible to attain, but they all surely knew what it was. The moonshot vision statement was succinct, memorable and measureable. It was lofty but attainable. Each person clearly recognized how what he or she did every day in their jobs contributed – even if in just a small way - to the successful realization of the common purpose. In addition, the number of decisions at each level that needed to be correctly made, many of them through heated debate and endless trial and error, was staggering. In the end, as the three star voyagers were safely retrieved from the confines of their tiny capsule in the Pacific Ocean, the sense of a monumental team accomplishment, achieved through a disciplined, multi-year process, was incredibly obvious, palpable and gratifying to all.

Business leaders know that perhaps the most critical ongoing decisions they must make concern personnel. Do you have the right team in place? Do they have the requisite education, experience and skills? Are they well-trained? Do you trust them? Will they get the job done? How do you develop and retain your best people? It is said that legendary General Electric CEO Jack Welsh spent 50 percent of his time on people-related issues. NASA leadership chose well when deciding which three astronauts would ride Apollo 11.

Mike Collins was a 1952 West Point graduate who came from a distinguished military family. He chose the Air Force over the Army when given the option. Unlike his future Apollo crewmates, he was not a combat pilot in the Korean War, serving instead in Europe. His overseas obligation complete, he applied to be a test pilot at Edwards Air Force Base in California, and though a long shot, he was accepted into the program in the late summer of 1960. Collins was captivated by the achievements of the first group of NASA astronauts, so threw his hat into the ring to be considered for the second team. He was rejected. He persisted, however, and was finally selected, along with Buzz Aldrin, in the third group.

All of the men of the Gemini program were assigned an area of specialization in which they were expected to become expert. Collins concentrated on space suits and spacewalks, known as extravehicular activity, or EVA. He soon realized that the work on spacesuits was tremendously important, a life-or-death proposition. The spacesuit, made of fabric and rubber, represented the only layer of protection between a human being and the unforgiving harshness of space. The study of EVA came in handy when, from July 18 to 21, 1966, Collins, along with colleague John Young, manned the Gemini 10 mission. In addition to setting a new altitude record and undertaking numerous scientific, technological and medical experiments, this was the first flight to conduct two rendezvous and docking tests with a target vehicle, known as *Agena*. Collins became the first astronaut to transfer from one spacecraft to another while in orbit, as well as the first to execute two EVAs. All of this represented excellent preparation for the Apollo 11 mission to come.

Edwin "Buzz" Aldrin was also a West Pointer, finishing third in the class of 1951. Upon graduation, Aldrin accepted his Air Force commission and deployed to Korea, where he flew 65 combat missions and shot down two enemy aircraft. In 1959, after postings in Europe and at Nellis Air Force base in Nevada, Aldrin entered the Massachusetts Institute of Technology to pursue a PhD. While there, like so many other Americans, he became inspired by John Kennedy's stirring vision of a Moon landing. He desperately wanted to be an astronaut, but lacked a key qualification. Aldrin reflected later, "The country was swept up in the space program, and I wanted to be a part of it. But NASA retained its requirement that astronauts have a diploma from military test-pilot school – not one of my credentials. Since I knew that the Moon landing program Kennedy had described would need astronauts with skills other than the ones they drummed into you at test pilot school, I opted for another eighteen months of intensive work on a doctorate in astronautics, specializing in manned orbital rendezvous."

Aldrin made a smart bet. Upon receiving his doctorate, he applied to be in the second group of astronauts but was, unsurprisingly, rejected for lack of test pilot experience. Like Collins, he too persisted. When NASA dropped the test pilot prerequisite, Aldrin put his name in the running once more. He received a call from astronaut manager Deke Slayton, who said, "We'd sure like you to become an astronaut." "Shoot Deke, I'd be delighted to accept," replied Aldrin. He was the only PhD in the astronaut corps, and his NASA specialty, for which he was so uniquely and thoroughly prepared, became orbital rendezvous techniques. His fellow astronauts dubbed him "Dr. Rendezvous." In November 1966, Aldrin flew on Gemini 12, the final crewed Gemini flight, during which he spent five hours and 30 minutes spacewalking over three periods of EVA. Aldrin was clearly a formidable talent in the astronaut corps.

Could there possibly be a more All-American name for the first human being to step onto the Moon than Neil Armstrong? He was a former Navy flier who completed 78 combat missions in Korea, including one which ended with him bailing out of his crippled fighter. He left the Navy and earned a B.S. in aeronautical engineering from Purdue University. He worked briefly at the Lewis Flight Propulsion Laboratory in Cleveland, Ohio (later a NASA facility), then transferred to test pilot school at Edwards Air Force Base. Armstrong was fascinated by high-performance aircraft and he knew Edwards was the place to be. He was an employee of NASA's civilian precursor, the National Advisory Committee for Aeronautics (NACA). At NACA, Armstrong was in a very real sense in astronaut training; he flew the famous North American X-15 rocket plane while readying himself to participate in two Air Force spaceflight programs, one called Man in Space Soonest and the other known as Project Dyna-Soar. These programs were ultimately canceled as NASA expanded its scope of responsibility. When the call went out for a second team of astronauts, Armstrong applied and was accepted in September 1962.

Armstrong was NASA's first civilian astronaut, making his inaugural spaceflight as command pilot of Gemini 8 in March 1966. This mission performed the first docking of two spacecraft in orbit, but also had to be aborted as a result of an in-flight system failure; Armstrong and fellow astronaut David Scott returned safely to Earth. While the two men received some criticism for what had transpired, two weeks after the fact a Mission Evaluation Team "positively ruled out" pilot error as a cause for the emergency. Manned Spacecraft Center director Bob Gilruth concluded: "In fact, the crew demonstrated remarkable piloting skill in overcoming this very serious problem and bringing the spacecraft to a safe landing." If anything, NASA brass now had even greater confidence in Armstrong's abilities, and he would most certainly be given the opportunity to command a future mission.

One of the most critical decisions that NASA leadership would need to make revolved around the fundamental question: *Just exactly how will we propel astronauts to the surface of the Moon and then return them safely to Earth?* This was indeed a simple question; its answer was anything but.

There were two competing theories early on. The first came to be known as the Direct Ascent method. The idea was that an enormously powerful rocket would launch a single lander that would fly to the Moon, descend upon its surface, and return to Earth without jettisoning stages along the way. NASA had not yet attempted rendezvous and docking procedures, so the Direct Ascent approach was deemed by many the simplest solution. The downside was that a massive rocket, larger and with more thrust by far than anything NASA had ever built, would be required. This rocket would be called Nova.

The eminent Werner von Braun, along with many others, favored a more complicated idea, called Earth Orbit Rendezvous, or EOR. According to this method, the Saturn 1 rocket would execute multiple flights into orbit, where a spacecraft would be assembled in stages, and then directed to a landing on the Moon. This approach involved a tricky process of rendezvous, docking and assembly of components in space, a series of steps that no one at the time was sure could be successfully completed.

Both techniques held in common that the lunar landing would be achieved by some form of a spacecraft with propulsion and landing capabilities. The astronauts would sit on top of the craft in a self-contained capsule and then be lowered to the Moon tail first, coming down softly on a sturdy set of legs. The craft would support the astronauts throughout their exploration of the surface, then lift off and return home to Earth. The key point of disagreement was whether that spacecraft should be assembled on the ground or in orbit. These were the two best options that NA-

SA's keenest scientific and engineering minds could conceive, until a third possibility emerged.

The conception and selling of the Lunar Orbit Rendezvous (LOR) method represents a dramatic example of how one creative, persistent person, even one who labors in relative anonymity in the middle levels of an organization, can have a massive impact on history. John Houbolt was an obscure rendezvous and orbital design expert working out of NASA's facility in Langley, Virginia. Houbolt recognized the reality that no matter which concept prevailed, Direct Ascent or EOR, the only part of the spacecraft that would return to Earth would be the tiny Apollo capsule. Whether the Nova superbooster carried a gigantic launcher assembled on the ground, or that launcher was built step-by-step in orbit, every other stage but the capsule would ultimately need to be jettisoned prior to the return to Earth.

Building on ideas that had been expressed by others in the past, Houbolt pondered the most efficient design for disposable pieces that would maximize power yet minimize weight. He prepared detailed calculations around the possibility of a separate, dedicated lunar lander. His LOR method would launch two pared-down spacecraft: a capsule with propulsion capabilities and a lunar lander. Three astronauts would orbit the Moon in a command module (CM), with two of them then moving to the lunar lander, while the third remained in orbit. The craft which eventually came to be called the lunar module (LM) would then descend to the Moon. Exploration of the lunar surface complete, the LM would separate from the landing stage, go back into orbit, rendezvous and dock with the CM. This was a seemingly elegant, efficient way to eliminate weight and save fuel. Yet the plan terrified many engineers, who believed it was far too complex in its requirements for multiple rendezvous and docking procedures, something that NASA did not yet know how to do.

Houbolt nevertheless refused to give up, badgering anyone who would listen, including officials at the very top of NASA's bureaucratic hierarchy. He gained a reputation in some circles as a bit of a crank. A key breakthrough came when Werner von Braun, who had previously advocated for the EOR approach, came to see the compelling logic of Houbolt's conclusions. Von Braun became convinced that the LOR approach had many advantages and was no more dangerous than any other method. With von Braun's enthusiastic support, Houbolt won the day. The powers that be at NASA selected LOR as the best answer to that vexing question concerning how to propel astronauts to the Moon and return them safely home again.

●❯❯〉○❮❮❮●

Gene Kranz, flight director for Apollo 11, once observed, "A space mission will never be routine because you're putting three humans on top of an enormous amount of high explosive." Michael Collins described the sensation of departing for the Moon, as he and colleagues Neil Armstrong and Buzz Aldrin sat atop the Saturn V, the most powerful rocket in human history, first thing in the morning on July 16, 1969: "At nine seconds before lift-off, the five huge first-stage rockets leisurely ignite, their thrust level is systematically raised to full power, and the hold-down clamps are released at T-zero. We are off! And do we know it, not just because the world is yelling 'Lift-off' in our ears, but because the seats of our pants tell us so! Trust your instruments, not your body, the modern pilot is always told, but this beast is best felt. Shake, rattle, and roll! Noise, yes, lots of it, but mostly motion, as we are thrown left and right against our straps in spasmodic little jerks... I breathe easier as the ten-second mark passes and the rocket seems to relax a bit also, as both the noise and the motions subside noticeably."

The five F-1 engines shut down after two-and-a-half minutes, then Armstrong gave the command and the first stage fell away in spectacular, fiery fashion into the Atlantic. The S-II stage's powerful engines took over and the rocket continued its ascent. The S-II's engines shut down nine minutes in, and the second stage also dropped to the ocean far below. The next stage, S-IVB, fired up its single J-2 rocket for a two-minute burst of thrust that put Apollo 11 into its proper orbital trajectory. Armstrong confirmed completion of the S-IVB burn to mission control: "Shutdown." "Apollo 11," came the response, "this is Houston. You are confirmed go for orbit."

After just over two hours and 40 minutes of flight time, with all systems checking out and one-and-a-half orbits of the Earth complete, Collins executed a critically important step in the process, which he had practiced countless times in a simulator. It was called the Transposition and Docking Maneuver. Collins detached *Columbia*, the Command Module, from the S-IVB rocket stage, pulling ahead of it. The Lunar Module, *Eagle*, had been in a fixed position seated nearly atop the S-IVB stage. In a tricky procedure that lasted almost ten minutes, Collins spun *Columbia* carefully around 180 degrees and locked in to *Eagle's* docking port. Just short of one hour later, after fully pressurizing the LM, Collins continued in the driver's seat and separated the LM from the S-IVB, which shortly thereafter dropped away from the CM into a forever orbit around the sun. With that, the three explorers were on their way to the

Moon, traveling at a speed of more than 10,000 miles per hour.

Over almost four days, the mission proceeded without a hitch as the CM/LM coasted toward the Moon. Early on, the astronauts took time to clean up, eat and rest. They sent their first television transmission back to Earth, as millions of viewers the world over sat glued to their screens. Collins took the pilot's seat again after 26 hours to perform a maneuver involving the firing of the CM's engine to attain the correct trajectory for a smooth entry into the lunar orbit. Just over 60 hours into the journey the ship reached a point, called the equigravisphere, where the Moon's gravitational power became greater than the Earth's, thereby actively pulling Apollo 11 ever nearer the ultimate goal.

As the crew began to close in on the Moon, they strapped themselves securely in place in preparation for the engine burn that would put them in proper orbit, 60 miles above the lunar surface. The spacecraft's engine now faced in the direction of travel, and the ship would soon pass the edge of the Moon, known as the lunar limb, and then go to the far side, where radio contact would be blocked. Mission Control sent them on their way: "Apollo 11, this is Houston. All your systems are looking good going around the corner, and we'll see you on the other side. Over." There, they would fire their rocket engine, as Mission Control waited nervously for them to emerge safely from the quiet darkness. Gene Kranz said later, "There was a degree of seriousness in mission control that I hadn't even seen in training. That was when you realized this was the real deal: today, we land on the Moon."

Armstrong and Aldrin climbed into the LM, said farewell to Collins, and detached from the CM. They were soon beset by a series of problems. Radio communication became intermittent at best. "It was up to me to decide whether to make the go/no-go [decision] and continue the descent to the Moon," recalled Kranz. At the point of no return, Kranz checked in with his flight controllers, who unanimously said "go." Now an issue developed with the spacecraft's guidance computer, which began to trigger a series of alarms. The crew was concerned. "It was disturbing and distracting and we didn't know what it meant," said Aldrin. As they approached the surface, the astronauts looked out the window and realized that the area they surveyed beneath them did not look familiar. The terrain contained a number of huge boulders that would have destroyed the *Eagle* had they landed there. "I think we may be a little long," said Armstrong, surmising that they had passed by their planned landing site. He took manual control of the *Eagle*, activating thrusters that took them out of harm's way. But now fuel ran dangerously low, and they needed to touch down immediately. Kranz said, "We'd never been this close in training. We started a stopwatch running, with a controller calling off seconds of fuel remaining." With 13 seconds to go before the tank hit empty, the LM gently settled upon the Moon. Armstrong radioed Mission Control: "Houston, Tranquility Base here. The *Eagle* has landed."

Neil Armstrong became the first person to step onto the Moon at 10:56:15 pm EST, four days, 13 hours, 24 minutes, and 20 seconds into the mission, according to NASA's official press statement. He spoke the immortal words: "That's one small step for [a] man, one giant leap for mankind." Nobody heard the missing 'a'; either he forgot to say it, or he did and it was lost in transmission. Later, Armstrong listened to the radio communication tapes. As quoted in James Hansen's book, *First Man: The Life of Neil A. Armstrong*, he said, "As I have listened to it, it doesn't sound like there was time there for the word to be there. On the other hand, I think that reasonable people will realize that I didn't intentionally make an inane statement, and that certainly the 'a' was intended because that's the only way the statement makes any sense. So I would hope that history would grant me leeway for dropping the syllable and understand that it was certainly intended, even if it wasn't said – although it actually might have been." He was asked how the statement should be quoted. He responded, perhaps with a smile on his face, "They can put it in parentheses." Any confusion regarding first words proved of little consequence in light of the magnitude of the achievement. The "giant leap for mankind," which had been almost a decade in the making, had finally been realized.

When Buzz Aldrin followed Armstong down, he sensed "magnificent desolation." "You could look at the horizon," he said, "and see very clearly because there was no atmosphere, there was no haze or anything." Over the course of 21 hours and 36 minutes exploring the Moon, the astronauts gathered rock samples, set up various scientific experiments, took pictures, erected an American flag (with great difficulty), and fielded a call from President Richard Nixon. They climbed back into the LM, located and jury-rigged a fix for a broken circuit breaker switch, then lifted off to rendezvous with their friend Michael Collins, intercepting him as he orbited the Moon, 60 miles above. Collins remembered years later, "I was absolutely delighted to see 'em. I was about to kiss Buzz Aldrin on the forehead. And I decided maybe no, no, I think the history books wouldn't like that. So, sure. It was a wonderful instant in time. But, okay, we had to get the command module cranked up. Get rid of the *Eagle*. Burn the engine. Get out of lunar orbit." They accomplished all of those things and journeyed safely home, exhausted but exhilarated, to a very well-deserved hero's reception.

As an example of establishing and achieving a lofty common purpose, the Apollo 11 mission can hardly be matched in American history. This incredible adventure story is also unparalleled as an example of a team united, determined to make sound decisions at every level, in the spirit of serving a greater good. Glynn Lunney, an employee of NASA since its inception in 1958 and a flight director for both the Gemini and Apollo programs, reflected on the totality of the experience: "But in the whole course of it, the program had this energy that was pervasive. We had been involved in this whole thing for a long time – over eight years. There was a powerful sense of people wanting to pull off the Apollo Moon landing and return within the decade, meeting the challenge and the goal."

Moonshot challenges that align with the right purpose are galvanizing.

ALBERT BOURLA

CHAPTER SIX

CASE STUDIES: COMMON PURPOSE

In 2019, Gallup conducted a poll in which it asked Americans to rank two dozen industries, from most to least favorable. The pharmaceutical industry finished dead last. That same year, Big Pharma CEO's were brought to task in testimony before Congress for price gouging, among other sins. Legislators threatened price controls. The perception of its failure to make drugs affordable for ordinary people, lack of innovation, over-emphasis on marketing versus research, slow pace in bringing new products to market, and poor business returns had long hampered the drug-making industry. Because of strict regulation and legitimate concerns over safety, new vaccines required extended developmental timelines, often taking as long as a decade to go to market. But during the coronavirus pandemic, Big Pharma surprised everyone by achieving the impossible. In just over a year from the time of discovery of the virus, government regulators in the U.S. authorized several vaccines for emergency use. No company better exemplified the establishment of a lofty common purpose, the mustering of a total team effort, and accomplishment of the goal in record time, than Pfizer.

Albert Bourla became CEO of Pfizer in early 2019. Raised in a Jewish family in Greece, Bourla was trained as a veterinarian with a PhD in the biology of reproduction. He joined Pfizer in 1993, starting in the animal health division, and gradually made his way up the ladder while working in eight different cities and five countries. He became a group president in 2014, chief operating officer in 2018, then assumed the CEO title the next year. In an article in the summer of 2021 from the *Harvard*

Business Review, Bourla said, "My exposure to so many cultures, my background as a scientist, and the diversity of roles I had taken on across Pfizer helped prepare me for my new responsibilities."

Throughout his career Bourla had maintained a patient-first mentality, measuring outcomes not based on sales but on the number of end users of Pfizer products successfully served. When he took the top job, he made a conscious decision to emphasize science and patients. He said, "We would need to focus on all stakeholders, not just shareholders, to create long-term value. We hung pictures of patients on the walls of our buildings around the world to drive that point home for our executives and employees." In March of 2020, as Covid-19 rapidly spread and the global economy began to shut down, Bourla issued a challenge to his team: he told them that they would "make the impossible possible." Pfizer, in partnership with a German company called BioNTech, would develop a vaccine to fight the virus in record time. Bourla's timeline was to achieve this goal, ideally, within six months, and certainly no later than year end. Experts scoffed. But the teams at Pfizer and BioNTech got to work.

When the virus hit, Pfizer was already deeply invested in infectious disease and vaccine work. The company had recently undertaken an effort with BioNTech to apply its German partner's most important technology, messenger RNA (mRNA), to flu vaccines. The leadership of BioNTech pointed out that mRNA vaccines, which are created synthetically by using a pathogen's genetic code, can be developed more rapidly than traditional vaccines. And speed was now of the essence. The two companies signed a letter of intent to go all-in together. Pfizer's expertise in navigating regulatory processes, manufacturing and distribution would combine with BioNTech's unique and promising mRNA technology to defeat the virus; the financial details of the collaboration would be negotiated later. Bourla said, "Saving lives – as many and as soon as possible – would be our top priority."

Standard practice in vaccine development typically involves testing the most promising candidates sequentially. Pfizer-BioNTech made a decision to work on potential vaccines in parallel, a financially risky move but one that would speed up the process. Vaccine candidates were soon narrowed down to four viable possibilities. Both U.S. and German regulatory authorities granted permission to conduct animal and human testing simultaneously. By May, phase one trials had narrowed the choices to two candidates. Subsequent phase two and phase three trials, involving hundreds to thousands of subjects, which historically can take up to four years, also ran concurrently. In late July, Pfizer learned that one candidate had moved to the top of list; it would require two shots, three weeks apart, but not only did it produce a strong immune response, it also generated fewer side effects. This was where the team would now focus its efforts.

Pfizer's formidable manufacturing processes kicked into gear. Trial doses would need to go to tens of thousands of volunteers, and when the vaccine was finally ready, hundreds of millions of doses would need to be delivered to all corners of the globe. The process required installation of new equipment and the development of never-before attempted methodologies at Pfizer plants in the U.S. and Europe. Pfizer engineers worked through storage and transportation challenges, inventing a thermal shipping and storage box so the vaccine could be shipped and held stable at subzero temperatures. The company immediately began production, betting that the trials would be successful. The risk was substantial and failure would be costly. Nevertheless, Pfizer prepared 1.5 million doses to be ready for a September shipment.

Through it all, Albert Bourla made sure that no corners were cut. He said, "Though our scientists and manufacturing teams were working harder than ever to meet the accelerated timetable, and we faced immense political and personal pressure, we remained clear about one thing: We would move only as fast as the science allowed." Bourla initiated an agreement among Pfizer and eight other Big Pharma companies that promised to adhere to the strictest scientific and safety standards in the collective search for a successful vaccine. Bourla was emphatic: "Speed was critical – but not at the expense of scientific rigor."

On November 8, Bourla gathered with a handful of members of his senior leadership team. The companies had run a "double-blind" study, meaning neither Pfizer-BioNTech employees nor patients knew who was receiving a placebo versus the actual vaccine. A group of independent data monitors met on that day to review the results of the clinical trial. They would convey their conclusions to a small team of Pfizer's lead scientists, who would in turn inform the leadership. Everyone braced for the possibility that the trial was a complete failure. In the alternative, they might receive direction that the results were inconclusive, and to continue testing. Finally, they might hear the news they desperately hoped for: the vaccine was safe and effective, in which case they would apply for immediate emergency-use authorization. After a tense waiting period, the scientists reached out and suggested a video conference. Bourla and team saw beaming faces when they finally connected, and knew that their Herculean efforts had paid incredible dividends.

The efficacy rate of the vaccine proved to be an incredible 95.6 percent. Pfizer manufactured nearly 75 million doses by December; more than 45 million had been released. In June 2021, the company committed to providing two billion vaccine doses to the poorest countries of the world, and partnered with the U.S. government to deliver at least 500 million of those doses as soon as possible. By October 2021, as reported in the *Wall Street Journal*, the Pfizer-BioNTech vaccine had proven itself as the world's vaccine of choice: "From Latin America to the Middle East, dozens of governments are turning to the shot. Australia is now offering the vaccine, after shifting away from competitors. Turkey, the UK and Chile are providing the Pfizer-BioNTech vaccine to people who took other shots.... Pfizer said it has shipped more than 1.6 billion doses so far to over 130 countries." Bourla summarized: "It took a moonshot challenge, out-of-the-box thinking, intercompany cooperation, liberation from bureaucracy, and, most of all, hard work from everyone at Pfizer and BioNTech to accomplish what we did in 2020. Organizations of any size or in any industry can use these strategies both to solve their own problems and to produce important work that benefits society."

What lessons did Pfizer take away that other organizations can learn from when setting out to establish and achieve a lofty goal? First, teamwork was of paramount importance (remember the 400,000 people it took to put a man on the Moon?). Bourla said: "Every single person in our company and at BioNTech – from senior executives to manufacturing and transportation staffers – was instrumental in the development of our vaccine.... I am awed by, and immensely grateful for, what all those people have accomplished." Second, the exclusive focus on purpose above all other considerations was key. Pfizer made an enormous financial investment in a very risky endeavor; the whole thing could have been ruinous to the bottom line. Nevertheless, "We drove ahead with mission in mind," said Bourla. "Still, even if we hadn't developed an impressively effective vaccine, distributed it as quickly as we did, and earned back our outlay, our decision to do the right thing would have been worth it for me, our employees, and the industry." Third, a lofty challenge in combination with a noble purpose can galvanize a team. When Bourla suggested the initial six-month target, "... our scientists [and supply group] were incredulous... They didn't think they could, but they ultimately found a way to make the impossible possible."

The fourth lesson learned involved the requirement for new ways of thinking in order to solve a problem they had never confronted before. Initially, when Pfizer teams presented leadership with proposed solutions, they recounted what had worked in the past. Leadership insisted that they engage in out-of-the-box thinking, which eventually developed into a habit and allowed the end goal to be reached. Fifth, the leadership team freed the scientists and others who were tasked with solving the challenge from bureaucratic and financial concerns. Money was no object, and because Pfizer took no funding from either the U.S. or German governments, they were without financial obligations to others. Finally, cooperation, especially in light of the crisis circumstances, was a critical factor in reaching the goal. Bourla explained, "Our work on Covid-19 with BioNTech began without a formal contract. In fact, the terms of our partnership weren't hammered out until after year's end." That did not matter, because both companies "... were aligned on wanting to move quickly to make a difference."

An April 2021 article in *The Economist* touted the rejuvenation in the fortunes of the pharmaceutical industry: "Perhaps the most surprising reason for optimism about Big Pharma's prospects arises from its burnished image. Many Americans had never heard of Pfizer and those that did probably thought of it as money-grubbing. Now the company is hailed by ordinary people as a life-saving innovator. 'Big Science is good, and Big Pharma now has a seat firmly at the table and a chance to be 'good' again,'" said David Frey, an industry consultant with KPMG. Indeed, a 2021 Harris Poll indicated that public approval of the industry had increased by 30 percentage points from the previous year to more than 60 percent. The Pfizer- BioNTech partnership serves as a terrific example of the mountains that can be scaled through cooperation and team effort when times are tough. "None of us know what we are capable of until confronted with the most challenging of tasks," said Bourla. "Our work in 2020 was just the latest and greatest example. So the next time a colleague says that something is impossible, I expect his or her peers to say, 'Look at what the Covid-19 vaccine group accomplished. If they can do that, we can do this.'"

● ❱ ❱ ❱ ○ ❰ ❰ ❰ ●

Will Steger is one of the great polar explorers in American history. Born in 1944 into a large Catholic family in Richfield, Minnesota, Steger felt the wanderlust from an early age. When tasked as a grade schooler with drawing a picture of himself, he created the image of a boy with all his worldly possessions contained in a hand-kerchief tied to the end of a stick that he carried over his shoulder while running away from home. As a young teenager during the International Geophysical Year of 1957-58, Steger became entranced by an article in *National Geographic* magazine that featured the exploits of Antarctic explorers. In his book, *Crossing Antarctica*, Steger said, "My eyes dwelled on pictures of crevasses and mountains. I knew then that Antarctica was a place I had to see."

Steger's many accomplishments include leading three unprecedented expeditions: the first confirmed dogsled journey to the North Pole without resupply, in 1986; the 1,600-mile south-north traverse of Greenland, which was the longest unsupported dogsled expedition in history, in 1988; and the first dogsled traverse of Antarctica, the historic seven-month, 3,741-mile International Trans-Antarctica Expedition, in 1989–90. Perhaps just as important, Steger has been an extremely vocal advocate for climate change awareness for decades, and has used his platform to argue that rising waters and other effects from polar melting represent the "canary in the coal mine" warning of other more far-reaching, potentially devastating global outcomes. He argues for immediate and decisive action from all of us in order to avoid the most catastrophic results. (Author's disclosure: Will Steger is a close personal friend - we co-facilitate an experiential leadership program based out of the Steger Center for Innovation and Leadership in Ely, Minnesota.)

The International Trans-Antarctica Expedition (the "Expedition") represents a fascinating and powerful example of a leader establishing a lofty common purpose the achievement of which would require an enormous, sustained, cooperative effort on the part of many people. In that spirit, the Expedition is also a case study in the importance of teamwork – in this situation, literally teamwork between and among nations. The grand strategic objective of the Expedition was to draw attention to the need to amend the longstanding Antarctic Treaty to protect the continent. In order to achieve maximum positive publicity the second, very practical goal was to successfully traverse the continent. Finally, in order to have the best chance to achieve their objective, it was imperative that the team work well together and stay on friendly terms with each other. As Steger observed early in the journey: "While we get along well so far, I remain convinced that the biggest challenge we face is concluding this adventure as friends."

In addition to Steger, the team consisted of five other men from different countries and with varied skill sets: Jean-Louis Etienne was a French doctor and accomplished adventurer who had skied solo to the North Pole. He met Will Steger there by random chance and the two men began to plan their Antarctic journey; Geoff Somers hailed from Great Britain, trained dogs, and had experience as a member of the British Antarctic Survey. Somers would be the primary navigator for the Expedition; Victor Boyarsky was a Soviet scientist who also had experience in Antarctica, collecting ozone and weather data; Qin Dahe was a Chinese glaciologist who would take regular measurements of Antarctic snow to determine pollution levels; finally, Keizo Funatsu, from Japan, also a dog trainer, would have responsibility for the health and welfare of the most important members of the Expedition: the 36 specially bred-and-trained huskies who would provide the energy and muscle power to cross a continent.

In April 1986, during a 56-day journey, as Steger made his way with seven teammates and 56 dogs toward the North Pole, he had a random encounter with Jean-Louis Etienne. Steger reflected that the Expedition "... was the result of a one-in-a-million meeting in the middle of the Arctic Ocean, when the path of my expedition... crossed that of Jean-Louis, who was skiing solo toward the same destination. We sat that night in a tent and drank tea and talked about our shared dream of going next to Antarctica. We exchanged phone numbers there on the ice, and after successfully reaching the North Pole we assembled this International Trans-Antarctic Expedition." The Arctic Ocean is roughly the size of the United States and Mexico combined. Steger told me later that the odds of running into Jean-Louis in a mostly uninhabited geographical area of that magnitude were so astronomically small that he considered it to be a miracle of sorts. It is fascinating to contemplate how often important historical events are influenced by or even directly caused as a result of small, chance happenings.

The two men reconnected post-North Pole and agreed on the overarching objective for the Expedition. The international treaty that governs Antarctica was on schedule to be amended in 1991. There were 26 signatory nations, and they would debate whether the southern-most continent should be opened for the excavation of supposedly abundant oil and minerals beneath the surface. At stake was the apportionment of the right to drill for these valuable natural resources. Steger wanted desperately to ban drilling and keep the continent pristine. He said, "While the North Pole trip for each of us was a personal best, this was to be much different... Hopefully, by drawing some of the world's focus to the seventh continent during our expedition – especially by engaging the curiosity of the world's children – we will help illustrate why Antarctica is a valuable place that deserves preservation, not exploitation."

The logistics for such a massive undertaking were incredibly complicated. Cathy de Moll, who during a long and varied career has been a teacher, communications executive, writer, and entrepreneur, agreed to become the executive director for the Expedition. In her book, *Think South: How We Got Six Men and Forty Dogs Across Antarctica*, de Moll describes the enormity of the task: "For some thirty staff in seven offices, scores of partners, and over fifty volunteers, Trans-Antarctica was a personal challenge that demonstrated our character and tested our mettle. We raised more than $11 million in sponsorships and donations, created an unprecedented joint venture with the Soviet Union, negotiated ships and airplanes, and arranged the complicated transport of over a hundred tons of food, dogs, and fuel to and from the continent. We built the sleds; managed publicity; trained the dogs; designed the clothing; skied alongside with cameras; packed the food; manned the radios; wrote contracts, press releases, and lesson plans; flew the airplanes; and embroiled ourselves in international politics.... Our message of cooperation was aimed at more than ten million children who followed the expedition and the politicians who held Antarctica's future in the balance: *through our differences we flourish and, with all shoulders to the wheel, we can change the world.*"

The Expedition's route would traverse more than 3,700 miles, taking the team from the western tip of the Antarctic Peninsula through the Ellsworth and Thiel mountain ranges. They would reach the South Pole, then cross a largely unexplored and inaccessible area to the east that would take them to Soviet bases at Vostok and finally Mirnyy on the far edge of the continent (Soviet cooperation was critical to the success of the venture.) Such a journey had never been accomplished or even attempted before. Steger, who is a serious and respectful student of the history of polar exploration, said, "Only a handful of men have ever penetrated Antarctica's interior – Norwegian Roald Amundsen, Englishman Robert Falcon Scott, Australian Douglas Mawson, a few others. No one had even considered the nearly four-thousand-mile route we were to attempt. While most of the areas we would cross had been mapped, no one had ever traveled them in the seasons we would. We knew little about the weather we would face, despite days of laborious research, because records of weather in these areas during the winter months are rare. For much of our traverse we would be operating primarily on assumptions."

The Expedition almost ended before it began. On July 25, 1989, at the end of a grueling, week-long station-by-station passage from Minneapolis to the Antarctic, the Soviet-made Ilyushin-76 military aircraft in which the team, their dogs, and numerous support personnel flew approached a landing on King George Island, 75 miles off the tip of the mainland. This was a fuel-laden plane that some had dubbed the "flying coffin," and the 50-odd passengers held their collective breath as they descended from heavy clouds and approached the icy runway. Steger admitted, "In all my years of adventuring... I have never been this frightened." When the plane finally touched down, roughly but safely, "There was applause and cheers as a rush of relief pinned us in our seats." Jean-Louis shouted exultantly, "We have arrived! This is Antarctica!"

The journey itself was grueling in the extreme, and the men and dogs experienced every conceivable range of polar conditions. Endless daylight contrasted dramatically with blizzards so violent that the team was effectively blinded, with all progress stopped until the weather improved. September was replete with storms that caused wind-whipped snow and ice to coat the inside of the men's mouths; they were certain they would suffocate from the effect. Steger related that in October, temperatures became so intensely cold that the "... windchills were at the limit of what a warm-blooded creature could stand. Any exposed skin on our faces froze." In December the Expedition triumphantly reached the South Pole, but their ultimate objective was still far, far away. January and February brought incredibly tough sledding as they became the first to travel through the endless area of inaccessibility.

In perhaps the most perilous and heart-rending incident during the entire expedition, only 16 days away from their end goal of the Miryy base camp, Keizo left his tent to feed the dogs and became lost in a storm. He was completely disoriented and, at around 6 pm, his teammates realized he was missing. "We quickly counted heads and shouted outside for Keizo, with no response. It didn't take long for us to begin fearing the worst." The team pulled together 350 feet of rope, anchored one end to a sled, then proceeded in a circle with men evenly placed along the rope, shouting Keizo's name at the top of their lungs. They completed multiple 360-degree swings, but weather conditions and visibility became worse; they agreed to resume the search at first light. The next morning, during their second sweep of the area, Keizo came into view, waving frantically. He shouted, "I'm alive. I'm alive." Miraculously, he had survived the night in a snow ditch he had dug, just 600 feet away from the warmth of his tent. Steger reflected on the near-tragedy in the immediate aftermath: "One of our goals from the beginning was to emerge from Antarctica as a team, as friends. As we sat this morning... and relived Keizo's lost night, I looked around at my five teammates and realized we'd been successful."

After the Expedition, Steger lobbied intensively, testified before Congress, and personally appealed to President George H.W. Bush. Ironically, the U.S. was the single holdout with respect to the Antarctic mining ban. But Steger succeeded in changing minds, and on July 4, 1991, President Bush agreed to sign a 50-year ban on mining in the Antarctic and to approve the treaty itself for another 30 years. In October 1991 the Senate ratified the new protocols. Steger said, "This closed, for me, the circle that began four-and-a-half years earlier in that chance meeting in the middle of the Arctic Ocean. The accomplishment set me on a path for the rest of my life: devoting my efforts to alert the world to the dangers of climate change and advocating international cooperation to stem the tide."

It is generally easy for a leader to establish a lofty vision. For John Kennedy to assert that America would reach the Moon in the decade of the '60s required very little actual effort on his part. But Kennedy well knew, as any good, pragmatic leader does, that to set a hard-to-reach objective without the capability, resources, will-power, inspiration, and teamwork to be successful, will result in failure and embarrassment. Will Steger understood that in order to positively impact the negotiations regarding the Antarctic Treaty, his team needed to complete the incredibly difficult, agonizing and dangerous traverse; they needed to shine as bright a positive light as possible on the as yet unspoiled continent. And to complete the all-important journey it would be crucial that the team remain on friendly terms throughout. In all of these goals, and thanks in significant part to Steger's visionary leadership, the Expedition was a resounding victory.

More than 30 years later, Steger still marvels at how well the team meshed: "We were all leaders, we all had skills, and we were all involved. We had a democratic arrangement; there were only a couple of occasions where I had to pull rank and make a final decision." In what is a critically important lesson for all leaders in any field, the Expedition team had spent a great deal of time just getting to know one another. They had all traversed Greenland together (except for Qin Dahe) in 1988, and so had acquired a good sense of how each team member would respond and perform in difficult conditions. Steger explained, "We had really developed a mutual love for each other; there was a genuine sense of caring and a willingness to self-sacrifice for the larger goal. The friendship and camaraderie that we had was so vitally important to the successful outcome. At the end of the day, the most important lesson is that through mutual cooperation and understanding, even vastly diverse teams of people can accomplish great things together."

a wide and diverse range of internal candidates. Next, management and the board agreed upon a fair and thorough process and specific goals, as well as developing an initial role spec. In 2017, Mastercard engaged the consulting firm Egon Zehnder to create a leadership program for all the possible candidates. In addition, the consultants would evaluate and recommend finalists and assess Mastercard's homegrown talent against external stars in the industry.

Banga came to agree with the argument that a 10-year run for him as CEO made sense. He and Haythornthwaite explained: "Succession wasn't a topic of conversation just for the two of us early on; we floated the idea of a 10-year stint with the rest of the board, investors, and employees at our town hall meetings. Why? Because when a leader has been successful for that long, people often stop pushing back against him or her. We wanted our best and brightest talent to be driven to help build a great company and, one day, to run it. And in an environment of ever-accelerating change, by a decade down the road we would perhaps all feel that new blood was needed."

In that spirit, the leadership team cast a wide net in identifying 42 men and women, from all different functions within the company, who had the potential to be CEO. Mastercard supplemented its already robust existing internal leadership development system with a "senior management excellence program." Participants were exposed to the board, given opportunities to present, and were assigned mentors, in addition to receiving personalized coaching and development training. Eventually, the most promising candidates began to emerge. By 2018, despite the fact that the company was doing extremely well and there was significant sentiment in some quarters that Banga should stay on, the transition process became even more disciplined and structured. Several iterations of a role spec concluded that the next CEO should not be merely a clone of Banga, but rather needed to be even more flexible and forward-looking in seeking to address future challenges. By the spring of 2019, four finalists, all of whom had profited from the process and were thriving as leaders, came to the fore.

The entire board was deeply involved the whole way through. They determined that they were looking for a leader who had credibility and character; technical understanding of Mastercard's complex business operations; international savvy; strategic capability combined with the ability to execute and deliver a business plan; and, not surprisingly, a strong social conscience. In February of 2020, just as the pan-

Whenever you see a successful business, someone once made a courageous decision.

PETER F. DRUCKER

CHAPTER SEVEN

CASE STUDIES: DECISION MAKING

"We want to get as many E.V.s on the road as possible. We believe climate change is real, and we the have the ability and responsibility to create a cleaner, healthier planet." In January of 2021, General Motors Chair and CEO Mary Barra announced that G.M. would completely phase out vehicles run by internal combustion engines by 2035. This was a monumental decision and historic change of course for G.M., whose only electric offering at the time was the Chevrolet Bolt, and whose sales of electric vehicles totaled only 21,000 in 2020. In its announcement at its technical center in Warren, Michigan, G.M. outlined a comprehensive strategy to produce as many as 30 different models of E.V.s by 2025. The company intends to spend as much as $35 billion on the transition through 2025. Affordability will a key factor, as G.M. keenly recognizes it is in serious competition with other automakers and especially Tesla, who currently leads the auto industry's transition to E.V.s, but whose own models have tended toward the upscale.

General Motors is an iconic American company. Founded in 1908 in Detroit, G.M. currently employs 155,000 people around the world, with 94,000 U.S. employees. Its primary brands are Cadillac, GMC, Buick, and Chevrolet. The company has recently experienced a number of challenges: in 2019, a bitter 40-day strike at U.S. factories ended up costing $3.5 billion in lost profits; when the Covid-19 pandemic hit, G.M. converted to making ventilators, which resulted in a two-month closure of factories; and the company, like many other manufacturers, has been adversely impacted by ongoing world-wide supply chain disruptions.

In 2021, electric vehicles comprised only two percent of G.M.'s total sales and generated no profit. To say that G.M. is betting its future on E.V.s is a gross understatement – the very survival of the company is at stake. A number of factories around the world exist solely to assemble gas-powered engines and transmissions. The transition to electric will involve massive changes for employees and in the company's factory footprint. The company is spending $2.2 billion to undertake a gut rehab of one of its Detroit factories, which will serve as the primary E.V. hub and be known as Factory Zero. Two more conversions of North American factories to production of E.V.s are underway. In 2022, G.M. plans to hire more than 8,000 highly specialized workers. They will bring on engineers with expertise in fuel cells, battery technology, vision systems, robotics, and materials science, in addition to an expanded cadre of electrical, mechanical and manufacturing engineers. The company is also looking for software developers and computer scientists. Clearly, there will be no going back to the good ol' days. Gerald Johnson is the head of global manufacturing for G.M. and is a 40-year employee. In a report from the *Wall Street Journal* in February 2021, Johnson said: "There has always been incremental change. This is transformational." Mary Barra's bold decision to go all-electric, made in consultation with her leadership team and board of directors will, if successful, represent one of the most consequential reinventions in American corporate history.

Mary Barra is the first woman to become boss of a "Big Three" U.S. automaker. As such, she is one of the most powerful, high-profile executives - of either gender - in the world. She was born in Michigan in 1961 of parents of Finnish descent. Her father was a lifelong G.M. autoworker and Barra herself began her career with the company when she was just 18, as a quality inspector; specifically, she was tasked with measuring the gaps between the fender and the door of various models. She was asked in a May 2021 interview in *Time* magazine about lessons learned from her parents: "Both my parents were born and raised during the Depression. Neither of them had the opportunity to go to college, but they believed in the American Dream and so hard work was how I was raised. You worked before you played. And there's a love of vehicles. Every now and then, he'd get a chance to bring a vehicle home, and the whole neighborhood would come over and my brother and I would look at every inch of it."

Barra is a 1985 graduate of what was then the General Motors Institute, earning a B.S. in electrical engineering. A G.M. fellowship sent her to Stanford University where she received her MBA in 1990. At G.M., she has served as vice president of global manufacturing engineering, head of global human resources (where she famously reduced the company's dress code from a 10-page document to two words: "dress appropriately.") She moved from HR to become executive vice president of global product development, then took on additional responsibility for global purchasing and supply chain. She was named CEO in January 2014.

Directly upon ascending to the top job, Barra faced her first crisis. She discovered that a faulty ignition switch in G.M. vehicles had caused accidents over a period of years resulting in more than 100 fatalities and numerous injuries. She immediately took decisive action, issuing recalls for almost 30 million vehicles and compensating victims to the tune of $900 million. Barra testified before Congress and apologized for the company's actions before she became CEO: "In the past, we had more of a cost culture, and now we have a customer culture that focuses on safety and quality." She retained an independent investigator to determine root causes for the tragedy. Barra said at the time, "The biggest lesson I learned, and I take it to everything I tackle now, large or small, inside of work and outside: If you have a problem, you've got to solve it. Because that problem is going to get bigger in six months. It could get bigger in two years. But it's not going to get smaller with time." The investigator discovered underlying cultural issues within G.M. including poor communication and fear of reprisal for raising safety issues.

Barra began the difficult work of changing the culture. She fired those responsible for the ignition switch fiasco, fixed the safety reporting process and created a safety hotline, so that any employee with a concern could easily and anonymously report a problem. She also turned her attention to G.M.'s serious financial challenges, reviewing each vehicle and ultimately selling the Opel and Vauxhall product lines to the European PSA Groupe. Sales records began to tumble under Barra's leadership. In a comment that reflects her humility and common sense approach to the decision-making process, she said: "It's OK to admit what you don't know. It's OK to ask for help. And it's more than OK to listen to the people you lead. In fact, it's essential."

The transition to an all-electric future will require radically new ways of thinking and working for every G.M. employee. The challenges will be daunting, but both manu-

facturing leader Gerald Johnson and Mary Barra are optimistic. Johnson said, "From an engineering standpoint, electric vehicles of course require a lot of technology and innovation. The holy grail is finding that cost balance between electric range and the cost of a battery.... But I think where we will leapfrog others is on everything else that goes into the vehicle. We think we have an advantage with our supply base, with our ability to integrate our software capabilities. We also have an established dealer network that can help us."

Factory Zero will be a kind of E.V. testing laboratory; the learning curve will be steep and undoubtedly job functions will change. But Barra told *Time*, "We already build electric vehicles. So we have training programs for people to understand the difference between an E.V. and an internal combustion engine. And we have an incredibly capable and skilled workforce. So, will work change? Yes, but work changes every day. A lot of the skills can be very transferable." Should G.M.'s workers be worried about their job status? No, said Johnson: "I think every G.M. employee should be excited about what we're doing. Because we see our E.V. strategy in total as a full-on growth strategy. We will expand. Yes, some job assignments will change, but we will have opportunities for everyone to come along with us as we make this transformation. There will be more work available in that future than we have today."

Competition will be intense and success is far from assured. Tesla opened a factory in China in 2019, and since then its overall sales and profitability have steadily increased. Tesla owns more than two-thirds of the U.S. market and sold close to one million cars in 2021. The company is sharpening its focus on more affordable vehicles; in 2021, sales of the Model Y hatchback outstripped those of the pricier Model 3. In October 2021, Tesla announced an agreement with Hertz that by the end of 2022, Hertz would convert 20 percent of its rental car fleet to Tesla E.V.s. Hertz's order for 100,000 vehicles pushed Tesla's market capitalization beyond one trillion dollars, an amount exceeding the valuation of G.M., Ford, Toyota, B.M.W., Honda and Volkswagen combined.

Myriad other automakers are thrusting themselves into the fray: Renault announced that by 2030, all but a small portion of its fleet will be battery powered; Nissan has been selling its battery-powered Leaf for more than a decade; in 2021 Ford introduced the Mustang Mach-E, an electric sport-utility vehicle – critical evaluation has been positive and sales have been brisk; Mercedes-Benz began in the fall of 2021 selling the EQS, a luxury electric sedan; and B.M.W. intends to roll out the iX,

an electric S.U.V., in 2022. Finally, Europe and China have been heavily promoting E.V.s for years. The governments in those two enormous car markets are incentivizing consumers, subsidizing producers, and using regulations to increase sales. China especially is striving to become a preeminent force in the global auto industry.

When I consult with business leaders who are faced with an important decision, I frequently encourage them to gather as much information as possible in the process of asking three critical questions: 1) What is the worst that could happen? 2) What is the best that could happen? 3) What is most likely to happen? For Mary Barra and the team at General Motors, it seems the worst possibility is that they are simply bested by the competition, both foreign and domestic; that they build E.V.s and nobody buys them; that some better alternative to E.V.s presents itself; and/or that due to these or other unforeseen future scenarios, the bet on a bright, all-electric future destroys the company. In the alternative, the best outcome is that our collective mindset concerning the dangers of global warming changes quickly, and that people flock to E.V.s in overwhelming numbers. This would involve the playing out of a very real historical phenomenon described by economist Rudi Dornbusch when he observed, "Things take longer to happen than you think they will, and then they happen faster than you thought they could." The team at G.M. dreams about such a result, presuming they could keep up with demand.

Finally, the most likely possibility? This is extremely difficult to predict, but it seems highly probable that reality will end up somewhere between the complete demise of G.M. and E.V. nirvana. In August 2021, the Biden administration vowed to push sales of E.V.s to 50 percent of new car purchases by 2030. The White House was clear about the desired outcome: "... to drive the electric vehicle future forward, outcompete China and tackle the climate crisis." Business writers for *The New York Times* reported in November 2021 that E.V. maker Rivian, in the first day after its initial public offering, increased in value 29%, putting its market capitalization at $86 billion, $10 billion higher at the time than G.M. (this despite the fact that Rivian had so far only sold 156 vehicles). The *NYT* summarized: "The fevered buying did not come out of nowhere... investors increasingly believe that the market for electric cars will be enormous – and, for now, they are happy to bet big on companies in the sector that show promise and appear to have credible leadership." Also in November

2021, lawmakers in Washington D.C. passed massive infrastructure legislation with a number of key climate provisions. Among other initiatives, the package provides $7.5 billion to expand E.V. charging capabilities, which would allow drivers to take longer road trips without having to plug in their vehicles. Clearly, the momentum seems to favor the ultimate transition to clean vehicles, but only time will tell if Mary Barra's undeniably courageous decision to bet G.M.'s future will also turn out to be the right decision.

There is an old adage that the single most important responsibility of any leader is to develop other leaders. Among the most critical decisions that any organization undertakes are those that revolve around training, development and succession. In other words, decisions about people. Unfortunately, in my decades in the corporate arena, I have encountered very few leaders who actually truly take this principle to heart. One corporate boss who did take this challenge seriously is Ajay Banga of Mastercard.

Banga was born in 1959, the son of a senior officer in the Indian Army. As a youngster he traveled throughout his native India as the family moved from military station to station. He attended seven different schools before graduating from high school. Banga received a B.A. from the University of Delhi and an MBA from the Indian Institute of Management, Ahmedabad. He began his long business career working for Nestle in India, in jobs including sales, marketing and general management. He moved to PepsiCo, where he learned how to establish local fast-food franchises. He served for more than a decade in various management roles at Citigroup, including heading up the global consumer business. He had ascended to CEO of Citigroup Asia Pacific when he received a call from Richard Haythornwaite, then chairman of the board of Mastercard. Haythornwaite and his board were looking for a new CEO amid a global financial crisis, and wondered whether Banga might be interested in having a conversation. Though he was happy at Citigroup, Banga relished the idea of running his own show, and so joined Mastercard as president and chief operating officer in August 2009. He was named CEO in July 2010.

From the very beginning, Banga concentrated not only on the multiple decisions he would need to make to transform and build Mastercard's business into the future, but also on the need to systematically develop his team and drive a process

to identify his own successor. In a jointly-written *Harvard Business Review* article from the spring of 2021, Banga and Haythornwaite describe their methodology for executing a strategic CEO transition. During their first conversation in April 2009, they write, "The imminent CEO succession was our focus, of course, but – believe it or not – we also discussed the next one: Before Ajay even had the job, we were imagining his replacement and both expressing determination that we should not have to hire from the outside next time around... Ajay was willing and able to lead Mastercard through the turmoil and into a digital future. We also agreed that if he was successful in the role, his tenure should last about 10 years, but that planning for the next CEO transition would be an open and integral part of everyday senior leadership development from day one. This was a soft promise at first, but it would gradually harden as candidates emerged."

Banga did indeed deliver spectacular results during his tenure as CEO. In the decade-plus that he ran the company, he delivered a cumulative total return to shareholders of 1,581 percent. Mastercard's revenue was up an annualized 12.7 percent during that decade and profitability reached 18.7 percent per year. Return on capital was 40 percent annually and the company soared from the 256th most valuable business in the world when Banga took over to number 21.

Banga generated these incredible outcomes primarily by engaging his people. In an interview in *Fortune* magazine in the winter of 2020, he said, "I'm actually an old-fashioned believer in capitalism. It's lifted a lot of people out of poverty. But what we need to do today is to reposition it for stakeholder capitalism – which is just capitalism with guard rails. And the first of those guard rails is to take care of your employees." Mastercard set up a plan through which 70 percent of employees receive a stock incentive award. The company further rewarded its people by beefing up retirement plans. Mastercard employees, for example, that save 6 percent of salary into their 401(k) or defined contribution plan receive a 10 percent match from the company.

Perhaps most important, Banga built a culture that emphasizes simple human decency. "I think decency," he reflected, "is the bedrock of defining what makes us human. Decency doesn't mean being nice to everybody. It means being fair to everybody.... And I say you need DQ – your decency quotient – when you come to work every day. Because you have to bring your heart and your mind to work. You have to care about the people who work with you, for you, above you, around you. That's

where inclusion comes in. if I can make it a part of my business, then I can bring the whole company to the party."

Banga certainly understood that he was running a large business, and without profitability nothing else would be possible. He made key decisions to build analytic, cybersecurity, data, and artificial intelligence capabilities, which now comprise one third of Mastercard's revenue. The company set and achieved a goal of bringing 500 million unbanked people into the digital economy by 2020. Mastercard has succeeded in connecting three billion cardholders to more than 70 million merchants, through a network of 40,000 banks and financial institutions, in more than 200 countries and territories. Banga talked about his focus on employees and giving back to the community, but acknowledged another part of the equation: "Of course there's always shareholders who need to be rewarded too. Because if you don't do well, you can't do any of this. You've got to do well and do good at the same time. It's not an either/or."

Mastercard has indeed done both well and good during Banga's time at the helm. In April of 2020, the company set a new objective of bringing an additional one billion people and 50 million micro and small businesses into the new age economy over the next five years. In the turmoil of racial and social unrest that followed the tragic murder of George Floyd by a Minneapolis police officer on Memorial Day in 2020, Mastercard committed to promoting financial security and small business in predominantly Black communities through a $500 million financial contribution and various partnerships with Black-owned companies. Additionally, during the pandemic, the company made a $25 million commitment, in partnership with the Gates Foundation and Wellcome Trust, to accelerate the development of anti-Covid medicines. At the time, Banga said, "You could ask what the heck is Mastercard doing in a therapeutic accelerator? Well, my view is, if I don't get to normalization of growth, I can't have a prosperous community around me. Without a prosperous community around me, this is not going to be a prosperous company."

Despite all the pressing demands of moving the company forward and community outreach, Banga never lost sight of the need to train and develop his entire team and, in one of the most important decisions he and his board would make, to choose his successor. By 2015, discussions around the eventual CEO transition resumed in a serious way. The leadership team had a very strong desire that the next CEO come from within the company, and so as a first step they worked to identify

a wide and diverse range of internal candidates. Next, management and the board agreed upon a fair and thorough process and specific goals, as well as developing an initial role spec. In 2017, Mastercard engaged the consulting firm Egon Zehnder to create a leadership program for all the possible candidates. In addition, the consultants would evaluate and recommend finalists and assess Mastercard's homegrown talent against external stars in the industry.

Banga came to agree with the argument that a 10-year run for him as CEO made sense. He and Haythornthwaite explained: "Succession wasn't a topic of conversation just for the two of us early on; we floated the idea of a 10-year stint with the rest of the board, investors, and employees at our town hall meetings. Why? Because when a leader has been successful for that long, people often stop pushing back against him or her. We wanted our best and brightest talent to be driven to help build a great company and, one day, to run it. And in an environment of ever-accelerating change, by a decade down the road we would perhaps all feel that new blood was needed."

In that spirit, the leadership team cast a wide net in identifying 42 men and women, from all different functions within the company, who had the potential to be CEO. Mastercard supplemented its already robust existing internal leadership development system with a "senior management excellence program." Participants were exposed to the board, given opportunities to present, and were assigned mentors, in addition to receiving personalized coaching and development training. Eventually, the most promising candidates began to emerge. By 2018, despite the fact that the company was doing extremely well and there was significant sentiment in some quarters that Banga should stay on, the transition process became even more disciplined and structured. Several iterations of a role spec concluded that the next CEO should not be merely a clone of Banga, but rather needed to be even more flexible and forward-looking in seeking to address future challenges. By the spring of 2019, four finalists, all of whom had profited from the process and were thriving as leaders, came to the fore.

The entire board was deeply involved the whole way through. They determined that they were looking for a leader who had credibility and character; technical understanding of Mastercard's complex business operations; international savvy; strategic capability combined with the ability to execute and deliver a business plan; and, not surprisingly, a strong social conscience. In February of 2020, just as the pan-

demic hit, the company named Michael Miebach, who has been described as a "global citizen, strategic doer, savvy talent manager, and constant learner" as CEO-elect. Miebach took over the reins and Banga became executive chairman of the board in January 2021. In a dramatic reflection of the quality and fairness of the selection process and their loyalty to Mastercard and its top leadership team, all three of the candidates who were not chosen remained with the company as of the spring of 2021.

Banga concluded, "CEO succession decisions are never easy. But they are made much less difficult if you start the conversation extremely early and stick to certain rules." Mastercard's process was thoroughly systematic yet flexible. They looked at a multitude of possible internal candidates, but they also benchmarked against external talent. Banga steered the action but with extensive help from his entire board of directors; together they looked ahead to the future in developing and refining the CEO job description. Most significantly, they invested heavily in the development of all the candidates, so that everyone emerged a more complete and competent leader out of the exercise. "In the end, of course," said Banga, "you want the CEO you choose to be exactly the right person for the job. And you want everyone else involved to accept that it was exactly the right decision for the company. Our hope is that we've achieved those goals at Mastercard."

PART THREE

APOLLO 13

Survive we did, but it was close. Our mission was a failure but I like to think it was a successful failure.

JAMES LOVELL

CHAPTER EIGHT

APOLLO 13: HOUSTON, WE'VE HAD A PROBLEM

Apollo 13 was in trouble. The boys were in the shit. A potentially catastrophic oxygen tank explosion had crippled the ship en route to the Moon and drastically altered the mission. Instead of the anticipated lunar landing, the objective would now become simply to return the astronauts safely to Earth, by any means and as soon as possible.

In the morning on Friday April 17, 1970, as the perilous journey entered its final stages and the world held its breath, astronauts, reporters, cameramen, family, and friends gathered at the Houston home of James Lovell, Apollo 13 mission commander, and sat down around the TV set in the family room to watch the action. Blanche Lovell, Jim's mother, arrived via a courtesy ride from the Friendswood Nursing Home, dressed to the nines and in a cheerful mood. Jim's wife, Marilyn, had not yet informed her mother-in-law that her beloved son and his crewmates were in peril. As far as Blanche knew, her Jimmy would soon splash down safely in the ocean and then come home, just as he had done on previous missions. Marilyn felt it important, for now, to continue to shield Blanche from the truth, so she set her up on her own in front of the TV in the den, apart from the vocal crowd in the living room who understood the reality. Marilyn thought that someone should sit with Blanche and explain away any disturbing comments she might hear on the broadcast. Neil

Armstrong and Buzz Aldrin graciously agreed to the task.

In his book, *Apollo 13*, Jim Lovell (with co-author Jeffrey Kluger) explains what happened next: "In front of the television, Armstrong and Aldrin flinched a bit [at some of the commentary] and looked worriedly at the woman sitting between them. But if Blanche Lovell heard anything amiss, she didn't show it. She turned to the handsome young men on either side of her – both astronauts like her son, but both no doubt just ordinary ones, or else they would be flying in space today and he would be the one following things on TV – and smiled at them. Armstrong and Aldrin smiled back." Sometimes, ignorance is indeed bliss. If Blanche Lovell did not know who her illustrious companions were, or that her son was presently in grave danger, then she was probably the only one in the world. They were all about to find out, Blanche included, how the story would end.

The Apollo 13 saga can hardly be surpassed as a prime example of our two leadership dimensions around relationships and trust, as well as communication, in action. Without strong relationships and trust throughout the team, from the astronauts to all of those back on Mother Earth who were striving to bring them home, the mission may have failed. Clear, open and honest communication was a second imperative; anything less could have resulted in disaster.

In addition to Lovell, the Apollo 13 crew consisted of Fred Haise, lunar module pilot, and Jack Swigert, command module pilot. Lovell, the most experienced member of the team, had flown in Geminis 7 and 12, and had been the CM pilot for Apollo 8. Haise, like most of the early astronauts, had been a military fighter and test pilot. He was the backup LM pilot for both Apollos 8 and 11. Apollo 13 represented his first ride into outer space, and he was to be the sixth human being to walk on the Moon, behind Lovell (as part of the successful Apollo 12 mission in November 1969, Pete Conrad and Alan Bean had been third and fourth to traverse the lunar surface.) Swigert was a former pilot and, like Haise, had been accepted as part of NASA's Astronaut Group 5, in 1966. He specialized in CM operations and requested the assignment as CM pilot for Apollo 13, which would also be his first mission. Ken Mattingly, the original choice to fly the CM, became exposed to German measles during training and, because he had no immunity, NASA made the decision to go with his backup, Swigert (Mattingly never did contract the measles, and was deeply disappointed at the time, but given what transpired with Apollo 13, he may have wiped his brow and felt fortunate to have kept his feet on terra firma.)

In an essay written for the book *Apollo Expeditions to the Moon*, Lovell recalls, "Looking back, I realize I should have been alerted by several omens that occurred in the final stages of Apollo 13 preparation." In addition to the fact that Mattingly was scrapped from the mission, there were problems in ground tests before the launch. These tests, Lovell relates, "...indicated the possibility of a poorly insulated supercritical helium tank in the LM's descent stage. So we modified the flight plan to enter the LM three hours early, in order to obtain an onboard readout of helium tank pressure." Finally, the No. 2 oxygen tank, which had originally been installed on Apollo 10, was removed for modification but damaged during that process. The tank was supposedly fixed and then tested prior to installation on Apollo 13's service module. In subsequent tests, that tank failed to fully empty itself during detanking operations. After one more repair, the tank remained in place on the service module. Lovell admits, "With the wisdom of hindsight, I should have said, 'Hold it. Wait a second. I'm riding on this spacecraft. Just go out and replace the tank.' But the truth is, I went along, and I must share the responsibility with many, many others for the $375 million failure of Apollo 13."

Apollo 13 lifted off, in what was perhaps a final omen, at 1:13 Houston time (or 1313 in military parlance) on Saturday April 11, 1970. "The first two days," Lovell said, "we ran into a couple of minor surprises, but generally Apollo 13 was looking like the smoothest flight of the program. At 46 hours 43 minutes Joe Kerwin, the CapCom [Capsule Communication – as part of each mission, NASA assigned an astronaut back on Earth to communicate directly with the astronauts in space] on duty, said, 'The spacecraft is in real good shape as far as we are concerned. We're bored to tears down here.' It was the last time anyone would mention boredom for a long time."

Fifty six hours into a so far uneventful flight, Mission Control relayed a routine request to stir the service module's fuel tanks. Swigert complied, triggering the stirring motor. As he did so, a loud bang reverberated throughout the ship. Flashing warning lights indicated that one of the SM's power circuits had begun to rapidly drain. Swigert reported calmly to Mission Control, "Okay Houston, we've had a problem here." When asked to repeat the message, Lovell piped in, again, with laconic understatement: "Ah, Houston, we've had a problem here." At that moment, the spacecraft began to shake. Lovell looked out the window and saw a jet of gas leaking from the ship into space.

On the ground, Flight Director Gene Krantz listened carefully to voice loops from his controllers, several of whom reported sudden issues concerning various warning indicators. Houston received telemetry signals indicating that one of the SM's two oxygen tanks was empty, with the second one draining rapidly. In addition, two of three batteries that provided power for the combined Command and Service Modules (CSM) looked flat. Krantz later described what happened next: "The reports and our experience indicated an electrical glitch. I believed we would quickly nail the problem and get back on track. I was wrong. A crisis had begun. Events followed in rapid succession, escalating and complicating the problems as the crew's situation became increasingly perilous. It was fifteen minutes before we began to comprehend the full scope of the crisis. Once we understood it, we realized there was not going to be a lunar mission. The mission had become one of survival."

Survival would require that the crew of astronauts rely on strong relationships among themselves and with the extended team at Mission Control, which in many cases had been built up over years of working closely together. Everyone needed to remain calm, and trust each other and do their jobs. Beyond that reality, it went unspoken that only with clear and honest communication going forward would the astronauts have any possible chance of survival.

With Apollo 13 more than 200,000 miles away from Earth, the specific technical problem came into focus. The team knew that the ship's oxygen tanks provided fuel and air; in addition, those same tanks connected with a fuel cell that charged the batteries. The aforementioned explosion (later analysis revealed poorly insulated wiring as the cause) had ruptured the fuel cell system, but it was still receiving oxygen. The team quickly shut down that system to preserve the remaining oxygen. Someone floated the idea of tapping into the independent battery systems on the LM (which had been dubbed *Aquarius*) to generate power, but that source was inadequate to the task. Lovell said, "At 1 hour and 29 seconds after the bang, Jack Lousma, then CapCom said after instructions from Flight Director Glynn Lunney: 'It [the oxygen level] is slowly going to zero, and we are starting to think about the LM lifeboat.' Swigert replied, 'That's what we have been thinking about too.'"

The consensus was that the crew could use *Aquarius* as a safe haven, even though it was only intended for occupancy by two astronauts. They would transfer supplies, shut down the CSM systems to preserve them for the return trip, then move themselves over to the LM. Fortunately, Fred Haise was an expert on the LM. Nevertheless, he later admitted, "I never heard of the LM being used in the sense that we used it. We had procedures, and we had trained to use it as a backup propulsion device... [b]ut we never really thought and planned, and obviously, we didn't have the procedures to cover a case where the command module would end up fully powered down." Not for the first time, the astronauts and Mission Control would need to be creative. As Lovell concluded, stating the obvious, "To get Apollo 13 home would require a lot of innovation."

As the astronauts prepared themselves to make the transition from the CSM to the LM, the team in Mission Control worked frantically to answer a simple question with a complex answer: *How best to get our boys home?* Of course, NASA had contingency plans for aborting a mission, but in the case of Apollo 13 those plans required a fully fueled CSM and jettisoning of the LM; neither of these was presently an option. Kranz and his team came to the conclusion that the best - and probably only - alternative was to send the spacecraft to the far side of the Moon, then to use the smaller engines of the LM to generate sufficient power for a return trajectory. At the appropriate time, just prior to reentry of Earth's atmosphere, the astronauts would then transfer again, from the LM to the CM (called *Odyssey.*) They would ride *Odyssey* for the perilous final leg of the journey home. This path was risky, Kranz acknowledged: "We rapidly went through the mathematics; the lunar module was good for two crewmen for two days. A quick estimate using the LM powered-down checklists and taking the path around the Moon left us at least thirty-six hours short on battery power."

Some at Mission Control advocated strongly for a quick abort that would provide the shortest and fastest route back to Earth. Kranz disagreed, and stated emphatically as the debate went back and forth, "I don't want to jettison the lunar module. We haven't nailed down the exact cause of the explosion or the extent of the damage. The main engine or its control systems may have been damaged. We need more time to work out the procedures for the return." The dye had been cast and the decision made. Kranz concluded the conversation: "We should hold onto the lunar module and go around the Moon and take our chances with the LM power. I believe we will come up with a plan that will get us home." Putting together that plan represented the next critical stage of work for the team; everybody was all in, because lives were at stake.

The first order of business for the astronauts was to make an assessment of what they would need to do in order to survive on board the LM. At headquarters in Houston, all four ground-control shifts also dedicated themselves around the clock to working various aspects of the problem. Even with three passengers on board, it appeared oxygen supplies would be sufficient. But water reserves were inadequate and electricity usage would need to be reduced and closely monitored. Lovell summarized: "We had 2181 ampere hours in the LM batteries. We thought that was enough if we turned off every electrical power device not necessary. We could not count on the precious CM batteries, because they would be needed for reentry after the LM was cast off. In fact, the ground carefully worked out a procedure where we charged the CM batteries with LM power. As it turned out, we reduced our energy consumption to a fifth of normal, which resulted in our having 20 percent of our LM electrical power left when we jettisoned *Aquarius*."

The water challenge was more serious. "We did conserve water," said Lovell. "We cut down to six ounces each per day, a fifth of normal intake, and used fruit juices; we ate hot dogs and other wet pack foods when we ate at all... Somehow, one doesn't get very thirsty in space, and we became quite dehydrated. I set one record that stood throughout Apollo: I lost fourteen pounds..."

While oxygen stores would be sufficient, the team quickly realized that the astronauts were in danger of a buildup of toxic carbon dioxide. The air they breathed would need to be scrubbed. Both the LM and the CSM used canisters containing the chemical lithium hydroxide to rid the air of excess CO_2. But the LM's supply rapidly became depleted, and the additional canisters the astronauts had transported from the CSM were incompatible. Again, the team would need to be creative and trust each other. Lovell explained: "We would have died of the exhaust from our own lungs if Mission Control hadn't come up with a marvelous fix. The trouble was the square lithium hydroxide canisters from the CM would not fit the round openings of those in the LM environmental system. After a day and a half in the LM a warning light showed us that the carbon dioxide had built up to a dangerous level, but the ground was ready. They had thought up a way to attach a CM canister to the LM system by using plastic bags, cardboard, and tape – all materials we had on board. Jack and I put it together: just like building a model airplane. The contraption wasn't very handsome, but it worked. It was a good improvisation – and a fine example of cooperation between ground and space."

Mission Control also busied itself with developing the precise set of calculations necessary to time the engine burns that would allow the LM to enter a return trajectory after passing to the far side of the Moon and back again. In effect, the idea was to use the Moon's gravity to swing the spacecraft around and hurl it back toward the Earth, like the action of a slingshot. The first step was to put the ship into the correct lunar approach so that it would be on a "free return" trajectory, requiring exactly 30.7 seconds of engine burn. Next, during the return trip, a longer burn would expedite reentry into Earth's atmosphere by 10 hours. Instead of the anticipated Indian Ocean landing target, the capsule would splash down in the Pacific. The astronauts arrived at the far side of the Moon on April 15, and all communication with Mission Control ceased for the time being. At that point, the three men were as far from their home planet as any human beings had ever been – 248,655 long miles away.

Kranz described the incredibly effective communication process that his team used throughout the mission to solve the multiple problems they faced: "In real time I used the same brainstorming techniques used in mission rules or training debriefings, thinking out loud so that everyone understood the options, alternatives, risks, and uncertainties of every path. The controllers, engineers, and support team chipped in, correcting me, bringing up new alternatives, and challenging my intended direction. This approach had been perfected over years, but it had to be disciplined, not a free-for-all.... With a team working in this fashion, not concerned with voicing their opinions freely and without hurting anyone's feelings, we saved time. Everyone became a part of the solution." In short, in a crisis - and even when there is no crisis - leaders need to set aside their egos and listen with an open mind to what the team is telling them. Great leaders encourage their people to challenge them, listen carefully, consider alternatives, and then take action.

The team from Mission Control faced a fresh set of issues as Apollo 13 rounded the Moon and prepared to go into its proper reentry trajectory. The LM descent engine would need to generate a second burn, this one five minutes in duration, in order to expedite the journey home. The burn would take place two hours after the craft emerged from the far side of the Moon. Just prior to the procedure, a problem emerged. The astronauts had transferred the CM platform alignment to the LM, but they needed to ensure the course they were on was accurate before generating the burn. They had a sextant-like device, called the Alignment Optical Telescope, which required only that they lock onto a suitable navigational star. Unfortunately, debris from the damaged SM traveled alongside them and reflected sunlight in a way that made it impossible to sight on a star. Lovell related how the issue was solved: "A genius in Mission Control came up with the idea of using the Sun to check the accuracy of our alignment. No amount of debris could blot out that star! Its large diameter could result in considerable error, but nobody had a better plan." The strategy worked. Lovell was elated: "The alignment with the Sun proved to be less than half a degree off. Hallelujah!" The team executed the five-minute burn with confidence. They were not yet home free, but they had been blessed with luck so far, and the journey continued.

Mission Control had made another decision early on in the crisis. Despite the considerable damage to the SM caused by the explosion, the wrecked craft would be towed along for 300,000 miles in the hope that its bulk would, in the frigid cold of outer space, protect the unsheltered CM's heat shield from destruction. The CM's systems had been shut down when the astronauts transferred to the LM, and now needed to be powered up again without causing further problems. This was a procedure that simply did not exist in NASA's playbook, so the grounded astronaut Ken Mattingly, along with others, worked diligently to develop and communicate action steps that would ensure his comrades would survive. Lovell said, "A most remarkable achievement of Mission Control was quickly developing procedures for powering up the CM after its long cold sleep. They wrote the documents for this innovation in three days, instead of the usual three months." When the time came, the CM regained power without incident, and the astronauts safely transferred over.

Just four hours before Earth reentry, the blast-gutted SM was successfully set adrift. Lovell observed that, "With one whole panel missing, and wreckage hanging out, it was a sorry mess as it drifted away." About one hour before splashdown, the LM was jettisoned as well. This was a risky task because it required pushing the LM away by forcing pressurized air into the connecting tunnel between the two spacecraft. Things could have gone very wrong at this point, as the two ships might have collided, but they did not. The entire team, astronauts and ground crew alike, felt a pang of grateful sentiment as the lifesaving little vessel called *Aquarius* peeled away into the cosmos.

The astronauts endured an extremely difficult ride home. Lovell said, "The trip was marked by discomfort beyond the lack of food and water. Sleep proved almost impossible because of the cold." One man stayed awake on watch at all times as they neared their destination while the others tried to rest. In the dank darkness of their power-short craft temperatures bottomed out at 38 degrees Fahrenheit. Swigert's feet had gotten wet, and he was without lunar overshoes. In an almost futile attempt to stay warm he donned an extra suit of long underwear as Lovell and Haise put on their boots. Food was ice-cold. There was a further annoying complication. Lovell explained: "The ground, anxious not to disturb our homeward trajectory, told us not to dump any waste material overboard. What to do with urine taxed our ingenuity." The crew utilized the limited number of pee bags on board, then did their best to stash them out of the way. But Lovell was "… glad we got home when we did, because we were just about out of ideas for stowage."

On the ground, Mission Control continued to work feverishly, but also needed to maintain clear and cool communication with the astronauts. Kranz marveled at how Deke Slayton, NASA's senior manager of the astronaut office, read the situation perfectly: "Slayton… had sensed the pressure and came on line with the crew. With just the right tone, his reassuring presence calmed our deadly tired crew. Deke was a pilot's pilot, an operator's operator, a straight shooter. Deke reassured Lovell, Swigert, and Haise that all was well with the procedures, and he kept up the chitchat as the minutes passed with agonizing slowness. Coffee was the substance that kept us going…"

Neither Houston nor the astronauts knew whether the explosion had damaged the CM's heat shields or the descent parachute systems. They hoped that the strategy of carrying the SM along for as long as they could had provided protection for these critical components, but they could not be certain. All they could do was wait and see. The world-wide audience stood by in nervous anticipation as the craft approached reentry. Nails were bitten to the quick as what was expected to be a four-minute period of radio blackout turned into an agonizing six minutes. Cheers erupted when Swigert's voice finally came through loud and clear. Everyone in Mission Control watched, more than a few teary-eyed, as the *Odyssey's* parachutes deployed. The astronauts were safe, and splashed down gently in the Pacific Ocean, near American Samoa, less than four miles from the naval recovery ship, the USS *Iwo Jima*. Within an hour, three tired, hungry, dehydrated men had been hoisted to the rescue helicopter and triumphantly brought on board the *Iwo Jima* to a joyous reception.

The *Christian Science Monitor* summed up the mission well: "Never in recorded history has a journey of such peril been watched and waited-out by almost the entire human race." The astronauts had no clue. "Nobody believes me," Lovell said afterward with amazement, "but during the six-day odyssey we had no idea what an impression Apollo 13 made on the people on Earth. We never dreamed a billion people were following us on television and radio, and reading about us in banner headlines of every newspaper published." In retrospect, Lovell was deeply appreciative of the team aspect of the mission. "I would be remiss," he said, "not to state that it really was the teamwork between the ground and flight crew that resulted in a successful return." Kranz concurred, saying that, "Missions run on trust. Trust allows the crew and team to make the minutes and seconds count in a crisis." Lovell characterized the mission as a "successful failure." But for strong relationships and trust, coupled with clear, precise communication, the mission might have instead been a complete and disastrous failure.

Trust is the glue of life. It's the most essential ingredient in effective communication. It's the foundational principle that holds all relationships.

STEVEN COVEY

CHAPTER NINE

CASE STUDIES: RELATIONSHIPS & TRUST

I t is hard enough for an individual to win the trust of others. It takes time. That person's words must match her actions. That person needs to do what she says she will do, consistently and over an extended period. Only then might people come to trust her. Given that, how much more difficult must it be for a business, with all its moving parts and in all its complexity, and whose primary reason for being is profitability, to earn people's trust? Not just the trust of customers, but also of shareholders, employees, and communities? How many businesses can you think of where the word "trust" pops into your mind when you consider that entity? This is a serious question for today's employers.

In November 2021, 4.5 million Americans quit or changed their jobs. This astounding figure represents the highest number in the history of the U.S. Labor Department's monthly report on job openings, and is reflective of a mega-trend now called, "The Great Resignation." Not only do customers and shareholders have a choice in today's marketplace, but so do workers, so trust matters. Fortunately, there are inspiring examples we can look to for guidance and to learn from. If we polled the citizens of the State of Texas, there is a high likelihood that the grocer H-E-B would receive the honor of being called "trusted partner."

What is today known as the H-E-B Grocery Company, LP, was founded in November 1905 when Florence Butt opened the C.C. Butt Grocery Store out of her own home in Kerrville, Texas (hurrah for a woman starting what would over time become a tremendous enterprise, especially in those days in the American South.) The current H-E-B designation derives from the initials of Howard E. Butt Sr., Florence's son, who took over the business upon his return from the First World War in 1919. Today, the San-Antonio-based company has more than 340 stores, with close to 300 located in Texas and the remainder in Mexico. There are 100,000-plus employees and 2019 revenues were $31 billion, making H-E-B the ninth largest privately-held company in the U.S. according to *Forbes* magazine, and the 19th largest retailer. The company's official website brags: "No store does more than H-E-B, where you'll find great prices, brands, quality, selection & free curbside pickup. H-E-B, taking care of Texans!" The famous Hall-of-Fame baseball pitcher, Dizzy Dean, is supposed to have said, "It ain't braggin' if you can do it." H-E-B can do it, as far as Texans are concerned.

My adult daughter, Anna, has lived in Texas for the past several years. She and her significant other, Paul Garner, currently live in Austin where Anna is a graduate student at the University of Texas and Paul works in restoration construction. Anna grew up in Minnesota, but Paul is a native Texan. I asked them both if they would please tell me what it is about H-E-B that people like so much? They sent an email in January of 2022, in the form of what I would call a joint communique. It tickled me so much that I have to quote them verbatim. I believe they speak for many Texans, whether transplanted or born and bred, as they extol the virtues of their favorite grocer:

1. *H-E-B is affordable, and their sales can be bonkers. Yesterday, a sale on bulk items had us taking home 1lb bags of nuts for peanuts.*

2. *Accessible: they are open every day and even during the worst times, like the freeze of mid-February 2021. Within the city, locations are never more than a 15-minute drive and they are often adjacent to bus stops and highways.*

3. *Timely and responsible response to the various challenges presented by COVID: employees were helpful and stores were open from the first days of the pandemic. An H-E-B Pharmacy even gave me [Paul] my booster shot a few weeks ago.*

4. *Quality of food: they have prepared foods, staple items, and decent produce, especially organic greens, and good meats that are often from local ranchers.*

> *H-E-B will work with ranchers directly and process their meats through H-E-B facilities rather than buy from larger meat processing companies like Pilgrim.*

5. *Reliable: they are usually stocked with all food essentials including home and pet care as well.*

6. *H-E-B provides employee tuition assistance, professional development programs, and they undertake charity efforts (Hurricane Harvey programs, etc.)*

7. *Central Market is a more expensive branch of H-E-B's. They have vast amounts of organic produce, a bakery, a fish market, and specialty foods from all over the world. Walking through these stores is like walking through a foodie's paradise.*

Wow! I need to book a ticket to Austin, visit the kids, and see this amazing store.

As Anna and Paul suggested in their joint statement, one of the most important ways that any partner can demonstrate trust is based upon how they respond in a crisis. An article from the journal *Texas Monthly*, entitled "How H-E-B Took Care of its Communities During Harvey," describes the actions that the grocer took in response to the disastrous hurricane that devastated Houston and other Texas and Louisiana Gulf Coast cities in late August and early September of 2017. Harvey was a Category 4 hurricane that generated 130-mph winds, created flooding, and caused $125 billion in damage. Nearly 40 people died. H-E-B was not particularly well-known for disaster relief (even though the company employs a full-time Director of Emergency Preparedness), but in the aftermath of the hurricane, the company deployed multiple trucks, mobile kitchens, water tankers, and disaster relief units offering various services to the devastated communities. Of course, H-E-B also made a monumental effort to keep its stores open so that people could continue to be provided with groceries and other essential supplies.

Justen Noakes, H-E-B's Director of Emergency Preparedness, explained the company's disaster response priorities: "We are focused on taking care of our customers and our partners, and the number one way we do that is having our stores up and running. My number one goal on a daily basis is, any type of natural or manmade disaster that could affect the way that we operate business, I'm responsible for bringing a solution forward. That includes hurricanes, power outages, boil orders—we were very active during the H1N1 incident a couple years ago."

More recently, in February 2021, Texas got slammed with the worst winter storm in a generation. Texas runs its own power grid, and the system came to the very edge of collapse during the blizzard. Millions of citizens were left without power, heat and water over a sustained period during perilously cold weather. Almost 250 people lost their lives. But through it all, H-E-B persevered – the people of Texas knew they could count on their trusted partner. A February 2021 *New York Times* article entitled, "Crisis Puts Grocer Deeper in the Hearts of Texans," stated, "The storm and its devastation have tested a notion of independence that is deeply ingrained in Texas, a sense that Texans and their businesses can handle things on their own without the intrusion of outsiders or the shackles of regulation."

H-E-B is known for its superb logistical prowess, and just as happened during Harvey, the company deployed trucks loaded with plentiful supplies of water and emergency supplies to citizens in desperate need during the snowstorm. H-E-B's secret formula is really not complicated. The affection that Texans feel for their revered grocer "... sprouted from bonds that have been nurtured as the stores have become established fixtures of their customers' lives and communities, offering affordable prices, good jobs, and support for school programs and food banks." Stephen Harrigan, an Austin-based journalist, explained, "It's like H-E-B is the moral center of Texas. There seems to be in our state a real lack of leadership, a lack of real efficiency, on the political level. But on the business level, when it comes to a grocery store, all of those things are in place."

H-E-B's Justin Noakes offered more detail around crisis response: "That goes back to who H-E-B is as a company... We have a long history in the state of Texas and being part of the state of Texas. It's one of those things where not only are we a retailer in Texas, we're a part of Texas culture and a part of who Texas is. All of our employees are from Texas, all of our leaders live in Texas. It's not only a matter of are we a retailer in the state of Texas—it's part of our makeup and our DNA. When you talk about these disasters and how they impact H-E-B, it's how they impact our home. We treat our partners and our customers as family... It's not only a matter of bringing our stores up as quickly as possible, but the sooner that we can provide relief and the comfort and the items that people need to return themselves to normalcy, the better off the whole community is. We look at it not only from an entrepreneurial perspective, but also from a community perspective, as well."

Finally, H-E-B has achieved its lofty status in an almost mystical way by virtue of tapping into what is unique about Texas. If you want to establish trust, connect with the people who depend on you in a way that resonates with them; that is easier said than done, but H-E-B is proof that it can be done. In an incredibly entertaining 2018 article from the blog *Eater*, entitled "H-E-B Forever: Why Texas's favorite store is the cultiest cult grocer in America," author and Texas native Priya Krishna explains H-E-B's enduring appeal: "The story of H-E-B seems unoriginal, as far as cult grocers go: A family launches a store in a small town a long time ago... That store earns a loyal following and expands throughout the region... It becomes known among its fans for its wildly dedicated employees (many have worked there for 30-plus years), top-notch customer service (only at H-E-B will someone hand you a freshly baked tortilla to snack on while you shop), and unique food products (hatch chile cookies!). Adoring public odes are published about it across the Internet. Long lines form whenever a new location touches down.... This tale could be told of any beloved regional grocery store... What's the difference between H-E-B and everyone else? Sure, it's ranked among the top places to work and is pretty ahead-of-the-curve with its mobile checkout (maybe that's why employees at Amazon suggested that the tech giant acquire H-E-B before it settled on that other Texas grocer)... But, really, H-E-B has just tapped into one of the most powerful cultural forces in existence: Texas pride."

Krishna explains that most people who are not from Texas do not understand Texas; at least that's what Texans think – and they don't really care whether they are understood or not. Texas is more than a stereotype of cowboys and ultra-conservative politics. "There's rural Texas, Silicon Prairie Texas, honky-tonk Texas, hipster Texas, Latinx Texas, oil-soaked Texas, Vietnamese Texas, and yes, gun-slinging Texas — just to name a few." H-E-B has somehow succeeded in becoming a reflection of Texas, in all its complexity, and a source of pride. Krishna says, "What's unique about H-E-B fandom is that its customers are ultimately loyal to H-E-B *in so far* as they are loyal to Texas. This is perhaps one of the most distinguishing factors between H-E-B and the other cult grocers: People love Publix subs, crave Trader Joe's snacks, and revere Wegmans' customer service, but H-E-B is a way of life." And despite their reputation for braggadocio, brashness and brusqueness, "Texans, on the whole, are open, honest, dedicated, and friendly. Maybe that's why H-E-B resonates so strongly in Texas. The stores represent Texans as they see themselves. There is no attempt to construct a monolithic image of Texas — or even to help people outside of Texas understand Texas. H-E-B is the secret that only Texans are in on. It's a retailer whose ethos is very clear: This is Texas — where the food is better, the people are more loyal, and the shape of our state is actually quite remarkable. *Y'all got any questions?*"

The well-known baseball manager, Leo Durocher, once said, "Nice guys finish last." He even wrote a book with that title. Durocher was a long-time major league player, coach and manager. He was notoriously cantankerous, contentious, and cutthroat. He believed that only scrappy, aggressive people with a bit of a mean bone would consistently prevail in the uber-competitive world of professional sports. But is he right about that? Is it true – whether in sports, business, or any other human endeavor - that nice guys (or gals) finish last?

A really interesting business case study is currently underway that will test Durocher's hypothesis. The enormous global enterprise that is Amazon changed leadership in July of 2021. The company's founder, Jeff Bezos, who is notoriously cantankerous, contentious, cutthroat, and uber-competitive, turned over the reins of power to a new CEO, Andy Jassy, who is by every account one of the nicest guys anyone would ever want to meet.

Bezos succeeded over almost three decades in building one of the great business juggernauts of all time. Like any number of iconic American companies, Amazon started in someone's garage (think Hewlett-Packard, Microsoft, Apple, Dell, Google, etc.) Bezos left a lucrative Wall Street career in finance with the idea that he would try his hand at selling books online. He was 30 years old. He set up shop in his garage in Bellevue, Washington, in July 1994. Apparently, he didn't even own the house; he was a renter. He spent 60 dollars at Home Depot on wooden doors that he fashioned into his first desk. He toyed with a number of different names for his new enterprise, finally deciding that the Amazon, as the Earth's longest river, would be symbolic of his offering of the largest collection of books in the world. His website went live in 1995, when the World Wide Web was brand new, and sales increased week-by-week exponentially. Bezos struggled at first to attract investors, but by 1996 he had received substantial financial support from a number of Silicon Valley venture capitalists. His ambitions, accordingly, grew exponentially.

Amazon's sales in 2020 were $386 billion. The company employs almost 1.5 million people worldwide, and is the second-largest U.S. employer, behind only Walmart. Its market capitalization is $1.75 trillion, making it the third-largest company in the world. Amazon has become, no matter how you look at it, a behemoth. Many people love Amazon. Others hate it. Some, like me, both love and hate Amazon – it's complicated. The breadth of products and services Amazon provides, inexpensive pricing, the ease of shopping, as well as the convenience of rapid delivery, especially for Amazon Prime members, are all astounding and unprecedented in the world of commerce. On the other hand, Jeff Bezos is an incredibly complex, controversial character – let's just say, at the very least, that he did not get to where he is by being a nice guy. And the creation of a global empire exacts costs along the way.

In his excellent book, *Amazon Unbound,* author Brad Stone sought to "... pose the critical question of whether Amazon and Jeff Bezos were good for business competition, for modern society, and even for our planet." In describing Bezos, Stone says, "Amazon's founder was now so many things in the public eye, all at once: an inventor, arguably the most accomplished CEO in the world, a space entrepreneur, a newspaper savior and swashbuckling proponent for a free press – as well as a menacing monopolist, the foe of small business, an exploiter of warehouse workers, and the subject of prurient tabloid fascination. Such a disparate range of responses was also on display in the varied reaction to his February 2021 announcement that he would devote himself more fully to new products and projects at Amazon, as well as to his other interests, by giving the CEO job to longtime deputy Andy Jassy and becoming executive chairman."

Whether any of us actually trust him or not, Bezos himself has at least some understanding of the principle of trust. In his book, *Invent & Wander: The Collected Writings of Jeff Bezos,* he even entitles one of his essays "Trust." He says, "The way you earn trust, the way you develop a reputation is by doing hard things well over and over... It really is that simple. It's also that complicated. It's not easy to do hard things well, but that's how you earn trust. And trust, of course, is an overloaded word. It means so many different things. It's integrity, but it's also competence. It's doing what you said you were going to do – and delivering. And so we deliver billions of packages every year; we say we're going to do that, and then we actually do it." Bezos obviously inherently trusts Andy Jassy, who has proved himself and done what he says he will do, over and over, for many years as the proverbial right-hand man. The founder would not have turned over operational control of his life's project and pride and joy to any leader other than one that he trusts will do an excellent job. But it is interesting to contemplate - and Bezos deserves credit for the boldness of his decision in not selecting a mere clone of himself - that the two men possess vastly different personalities.

Writer Nick Bilton asks the key question in his January 2022 *Vanity Fair* article entitled, "Down to Earth": "Jeff Bezos's handpicked successor as CEO of Amazon is in many ways his antithesis: understated, modest, and relatively unknown. But can Andy Jassy manage a $1.75 trillion company, its 1.4 million employees, and a seemingly inevitable regulatory onslaught, all while maintaining his nice-guy reputation?" Jassy grew up in Scarsdale, New York, the son of a successful corporate attorney. He played varsity soccer and tennis in high school, and remains a rabid sports fan today. He earned both his undergraduate degree and MBA from Harvard University. The Monday after he finished business school, Jassy became a marketing manager at the then-modest startup called Amazon, in 1997. He grew close to Jeff Bezos, four years his senior, and served in a number of roles early on. He became Bezos's technical advisor, a job which required him to shadow the founder full-time.

Beginning in 2000, Jassy and a team of colleagues commenced planning what would become known as Amazon Web Services (AWS). The effort involved the development of massive low-cost infrastructure that would enable Amazon to efficiently run its own retail operations. Eventually, through AWS, Amazon started to sell their significant expertise to external customers. Jassy took the helm of AWS in 2006, building it into a pioneer of the cloud computing revolution that became a major and lucrative component of Amazon's empire, generating almost 60 percent of overall operating profit. With tens of thousands of employees and total 2020 revenues of $45 billion, if it were an independent, AWS would have ranked 69th on the list of Fortune 500 companies. Jassy is known as a highly competent, laser-focused, detail-oriented, hands-on manager who demands outstanding business results.

He is also uniformly regarded as a super-nice guy. *Vanity Fair's* Bilton reports, "When I've written about other tech CEOs – Jack Dorsey, Mark Zuckerberg, Steve Jobs, even Bezos – there has always been a seemingly infinite line of former employees, old friends, or cofounders, usually those who felt they'd been wronged, who have been all too happy to vociferate in great detail how fucked up their old bosses were as human beings. When it comes to Jassy, though, I couldn't find one person who could – or would? – say a bad thing about him. (And trust me, I tried.) All anyone could say was how nice and unpretentious he is."

While at Harvard, Jassy was concerned about a fellow student who was studying hard for an exam and not taking care of himself, so Jassy left food outside his friend's door each evening. His sister (of all people, his sister would know if a guy was a prick or not and in many cases be happy to rat him out publicly) said that he was, "born nice, grew up nice, and is still nice to this day – maybe nicer." Jassy is also humble and entirely without pretense. A friend of many decades says, "He honestly doesn't give a shit." He's been driving the same beat-up 1998 Jeep Cherokee Sport since he started at Amazon. With all of this said, he's not perfect. One colleague asserts that Jassy is so low key and boring that "you'll want to gnaw your arm off when talking to him." He also has a level of attention to detail that borders on the manic. Some Amazonians regard him as a bit of a micromanager who spends far too much time in the weeds and not enough time on the big picture.

The picture of what he will need to manage going forward is indeed big. In addition to its many business challenges, Amazon has been accused of maintaining harsh working conditions in its warehouses and relentless demands on its delivery teams, including an insufficient focus on safety. A January 2022 report from Amazon itself showed worse-than-average safety rates in its American warehouses, but a better than average record than peers for delivery. In recent years the *Washington Post* (owned by none other than Jeff Bezos!) found serious injury rates at a number of Amazon facilities far exceeded industry standards. The company has been fighting sporadic unionization efforts among logistics workers for years – successfully so far, but time will tell. Amazon's very bigness – as is true with its mighty tech counterparts – has attracted the attention of government regulators and political trustbusters who would like to see these companies punished for non-competitive practices, if not broken into pieces. Among other things, Amazon is accused of acquiring information from third-party sellers to develop competitive products, for the purpose of driving those smaller sellers out of business.

All of these problems and many more will need to be addressed by Jassy and his team. It is too early of course to judge his tenure - the stock market tanked in early January 2022, skewing Amazon's results (along with most other large public-ly-traded companies), at least in terms of share price, downward. But in February 2022, Amazon announced its 2021 Q4 earnings, and they were spectacular. Profit nearly doubled during the critical holiday period and there were huge gains in cloud computing and advertising. Interestingly, Amazon's investment in electric-car maker Rivian Automotive added approximately $12 billion to operating income. Quarterly revenue was $137 billion and profits were more than $14 billion. So far so good, but the ongoing "nice-guy experiment" at Amazon will remain fascinating to follow.

What is the answer? Do nice people finish last in the game of life? Many women who are in the corporate arena would assert, and justifiably so, that they face a sig-nificantly more difficult time navigating this tricky game than men. There is a very real double standard in play. As the husband and father of three women who have each experienced enormous frustration and discrimination in the workplace, based solely on their gender, I am embarrassed and discouraged by the unfairness of it. If a woman in a leadership role is nice, she is frequently seen as "too nice," i.e., not tough enough. If she is seen as tough, people may see her as "too tough," i.e., a real "you know what." It is a seemingly impossible balance to achieve, for a lot of women.

Nevertheless, in my opinion, based on study and my own experience in a long corporate career, regardless of gender, a leader can be terrifically effective and pro-duce wonderful outcomes while still being a thoroughly decent human being. In-deed, there are numerous studies that confirm this fact. Executive coach and leader-ship expert Ray Williams has reviewed the data and come to the same conclusion. He cites several recent studies: research by a number of business professors, published in *The Journal of Product Innovation Management,* shows that project managers got much better performance from their team when they demonstrated honesty, kind-ness and respect. The authors concluded, "If you think you're being treated well, you are going to work well with others on your team." A study from Harvard's De-partment of Psychology, published in the *Proceedings of the National Academy of Sci-ences,* found that dynamic, complex social networks encourage their members to be friendlier and more cooperative, while selfish behavior can result in a person not being accepted by the group. The lesson: "Basically, what it boils down to is that you'd better be a nice guy, or else you're going to get cut off." Finally, Harvard Business School's Amy Cuddy has demonstrated that leaders who project warmth – even before establishing their competence – are more effective than those who lead with their toughness and skill. One of the primary reasons this is true comes back to our tried-and-true principle of trust. Employees, like all human beings everywhere, tend to trust someone who is kind.

Ray Williams summarizes the data: "There is convincing research to show a connection among leadership behaviors marked by altruism, kindness, empathy, and compassion - elements of being nice - generating greater employee engagement, productivity and wellness. There is convincing evidence that companies that demonstrate social responsibility and are nice to their employees and customers, thrive. It's time to seriously question the outdated paradigm of a competitive, dog-eat-dog business world, driven by competitive, ruthless leaders."

Two of the best bosses I ever had in my professional life were Gail Dorn at Target Corporation and Shari Ballard at the Best Buy Company. I learned so much about leadership – and life - from both of them (even though both are younger than I am). Both women were high-ranking, well-respected officers of these two big-box retail titans, and enjoyed stellar careers. Both knew their jobs inside and out, were demanding, and consistently achieved outstanding business results. Both were, each in her own way, tough (interestingly, though I'm not advocating this as a requisite leadership trait, both could spin profanity with the best of the Marines I ever knew.) They got your attention and insisted upon high standards. But they were also both funny, charming, compassionate, considerate, humble, and a joy to spend time with. In fact, dare I say it, they were both really nice people.

The single biggest problem in communication is the illusion that it has taken place.

GEORGE BERNARD SHAW

CHAPTER TEN

CASE STUDIES: COMMUNICATION

Quick: can you think of a business organization whose culture demands brutally honest communication? A company that not only encourages frank, open discussion of mistakes made and lessons learned, but even punishes those employees who do not engage in full disclosure? Perhaps you do know of such a cutting-edge enterprise, but it would certainly be atypical. Better yet, do you know of an entire industry in which this kind of communication is the norm?

The airline industry has experienced a safety revolution since 2009. Over the past 13 years, not a single commercial airline in the U.S. has experienced a fatal crash. This achievement results from a game-changing reassessment of processes in light of a number of deadly accidents in the mid-1990s. At that time, a diverse team of people came together that included high-ranking federal regulators and airline executives, as well as leaders from the pilots unions. All parties agreed that they needed to develop a new way of thinking about safety in their industry that would include radical changes in communication. In order to address the hazards of commercial air travel, this group of visionary leaders created voluntary incident reporting programs that encouraged data-sharing among the different airlines and no punishments when mistakes were uncovered. They clearly recognized that they had to do this: lives and the future profitability and growth of commercial aviation depended on it.

In his book *Flight: The Complete History of Aviation*, author R.G. Grant identifies the conundrum facing those who focus on ensuring aviation safety: "The airline industry has always known that its success depends on convincing the public that air travel is safe. This has never been an easy task. The drama of major air disasters impresses itself so intensely on the public consciousness – partly, no doubt, precisely because they are rare – that flying is often inextricably associated in people's minds with sudden and violent death. Yet measures to reduce the number of air accidents and aviation-related deaths may undermine the image of air travel as a normal, safe, everyday experience. The more safety procedures passengers are subjected to, the less secure they are likely to feel." The fact is, even before the widespread development of improved safety procedures, air travel was and remains by far the safest means of long distance travel. Whether people understand this or not – we humans are generally terrible at accurately gauging relative risk – we are all vastly safer and much less likely to be injured or killed in a commercial aircraft than we are in driving our automobile to and from the airport.

The year 1996 was a tragic year for aviation mishaps: there were 1,187 fatalities associated with commercial flights worldwide. Yet in that same year, approximately 250,000 people were killed in automobile accidents around the world, including more than 40,000 Americans. To be sure, air travel is much safer in some parts of the world than others, and small private planes represent a fiftyfold increase in risk to passengers. But as of the early 2000s, the chances of being killed in a commercial aviation accident anywhere stood at around three in one million. That means that an otherwise immortal human being could fly every day for 900 years before a fatal incident would occur. Those are damn good odds.

The road to better safety has been long and arduous. In the U.S. during the early 1930s, one person died for every 4.8 million passenger-miles flown. There were five fatal air crashes in America in less than one month during the winter of 1936-37. Such deadly high percentages would be entirely unacceptable today – people would simply choose not to fly. Fifty years later, in the 1980s, safety had improved such that one passenger died for every 300 million miles flown. In subsequent decades, however, records continued to be set for total air fatalities, for the simple reason that modern jets generally carried a much larger number of passengers per flight. In 1985, the worst year ever for worldwide air accident fatalities, 2,129 people died; just three incidents alone killed more than half of that total. By 2005, 1.2 billion passengers worldwide flew commercially, and there were 1,050 deaths; this number represents a tiny percentage of the total, but it was still intolerable to those who were striving to reassure the public by making air travel as perfectly safe as possible. They had to do better.

Grant points out that many people, serving in myriad functions, have contributed to the remarkable advancements in safety that those of us who fly benefit from today: "The safety of commercial flying is a triumph of organization and regulation, and a tribute to the professionalism of all involved in the aviation business, from those who make the airframes, engines, and avionics, through the ground maintenance staff and flight crews to administrators and air traffic controllers.... Considering what amazingly complex machines modern aircraft are – a Boeing 747 has about 4.5 million moving parts – it is astonishing how rarely they suffer serious faults. A modern jet may have ten hours ground maintenance for every hour it spends in the air."

Perhaps the single most important factor in U.S. carrier's vastly improved ability to protect passengers was the cooperative, multi-faceted effort undertaken by industry leaders in the mid-1990s. In 1996, 350 people perished in domestic accidents. At that point, there was approximately one fatal accident for every two million departures. The most horrific incident that year was the infamous fuel tank explosion during a TWA flight that sucked significant numbers of passengers out of the plane's fuselage – 230 people died in total. In the ensuing decade, the fatal accident rate was reduced by 80 percent, and safety has continued to improve. Today in the U.S., the odds of dying in a commercial plane accident are one for every 120 million departures. There was a passenger fatality in 2018, not involving a crash, when a fan blade ruptured in flight and killed a woman who was seated nearby - that is the sole death over the past 13 years. These safety percentages have become enormously better thanks to the efforts of a courageous group of pioneers.

When aviation leaders gathered more than 25 years ago to address the existential problems facing the industry, there was deep-seated skepticism that honest communication could take place without recriminations and punishment for self-reported lapses in safety. Trust would be absolutely necessary, but it would have to be earned. By the time the new millennium approached, leaders from the Federal Aviation Administration, the Boeing Company, unions, and the leading U.S. airline trade association had come together to endorse a unified safety process, based on shared data. Now they would seek to implement the plan. (Boeing has had its own set of serious problems in recent years as a result of two horrible accidents, one in Indonesia in

2018 and the other in Ethiopia five months later, and subsequent controversy involving its 737 MAX jet – a story for another day.)

In an April 2021 article from the *Wall Street Journal*, entitled "The Airline Safety Revolution,' writer Andy Pasztor explains, "The astonishing safety record in the U.S. stems most of all from a sustained commitment to what was at first a controversial idea. Together, government and industry experts extracted safety lessons by analyzing huge volumes of flight data and combing through tens of thousands of detailed reports filed annually by pilots and, eventually, mechanics and air-traffic controllers. Responses led to voluntary industry improvements, rather than mandatory government regulations." Ray Valeika, formerly chief of engineering and maintenance at Delta, described what happened when mechanics and air-traffic controllers set aside their hesitations and began to trust the process: "It was an incredible breakthrough. We actually patted people on the back" when they divulged mistakes. "But if management found it and you didn't tell us, then you could lose your job."

Some of the problems that came to light as a result of more open, honest communication included frequent pilot errors related to improper positioning of wing flaps during takeoffs, as well as inadvertent movement up and down from assigned altitudes while in flight. Fixes were frequently easy to make – for example, co-pilots were trained to pay closer attention to cockpit computers that controlled altitude changes and to double check with each other, out loud, confirming that data had been correctly entered into the aircraft's systems. Changes such as these were quickly and effortlessly implemented by the carriers themselves, with no need for regulatory mandates.

Again, technological advancements must not be underestimated as a boon to airline safety. Improvements in jet engine reliability, along with superior design and better components for electrical and other aircraft systems have resulted in easier maintenance and greater durability. But the simple yet powerful idea of creating open, honest and repercussion-free communication processes throughout the domestic industry has been the key. Pasztor describes the scope of the changes: "All told, the FAA has established a total of 10 voluntary reporting or data-sharing programs, covering everyone from airport workers to FAA engineers to technicians who maintain the agency's traffic-control equipment. Voluntary changes adopted in the U.S. include, among other things, more extensive pilot training to understand warning signs when flight control computers are set improperly or when airplanes are approaching an incorrect runway, how to adjust engine settings to prevent internal ice buildup and using cockpit radars more effectively to avoid turbulence in clear weather."

There is presently an effort underway to expand the scope of voluntary reporting even further, to also include those who design and manufacture commercial airliners. This presents an opportunity to continue to increase public confidence in commercial aviation, particularly after the 737 MAX crashes in 2018-2019. Steve Dickson, head of the FAA, said "I don't think you ever stop trying to earn the trust of the public." Other countries, who also benefit from improved technology but historically have not embraced voluntary reporting, do not have anywhere near a comparable safety record as the U.S. Many nations, from Asia to Europe to Latin America, are finally taking notice, realizing the error of their ways, and striving to emulate the American system. As head of the FAA from 2009-2011, Randy Babbitt was a former president of America's largest pilots union and a staunch advocate for the voluntary reporting system. He summed up the dramatic results of the effort: "The magnitude of the improvement has far exceeded my expectations... It's almost like buying a lottery ticket for 10 bucks and winning the lottery."

"I am a Black woman who doesn't play golf, doesn't belong to or go to any club, doesn't like NASCAR, doesn't like country music, and has a science degree in engineering... So when someone says I'm going to introduce you to the next CEO of Xerox, and the candidates are lined up against a wall, I would be the first one voted off the island." So says Ursula Burns in her wonderful memoir, *Where You Are is Not Who You Are*. In 2009, Burns was named chief executive officer of the Xerox Corporation, becoming the first Black woman to lead a Fortune 500 company.

Burns was born in 1958, and her incredible life's journey and rise to power began in a New York City tenement where she grew up poor, raised by a single mother who was a Panamanian immigrant and whose annual income never exceeded $4,400. Burns overcame the challenges of her hardscrabble upbringing and excelled; her mostly white male classmates and colleagues, "couldn't comprehend how a Black girl could be as smart as, or in some cases, smarter than they were." Burns was a brilliant student who graduated from Cathedral High School, then earned a B.S. in mechanical engineering from Brooklyn Polytechnic Institute (now New York University) and an M.S., also in mechanical engineering, from Columbia University.

Ursula Burns is known for, among many other talents, her extraordinary communication skills. Had she chosen to work in the airline industry instead of for Xerox, she would have been extremely familiar and comfortable with the principle of open and honest, even blunt communication. When she first became CEO, she convened the annual meeting of all of Xerox's sales representatives. She recalled the moment: "Eyebrows must have shot up during my remarks to the hundreds of Xeroxers gathered... when I admonished them not to be so nice to each other! 'The Xerox family suffers from terminal niceness,' I said to them. My basic message was that we had such an overly kind culture at Xerox that we at times supported each other's mediocrity... I have always been blunt in expressing my opinions, sometimes with good results, sometimes not. But it always stimulates discussion and saves time." Burns was not advocating fighting or screaming or throwing things, or that people should be anything other than respectful in their treatment of one another. "My point was that we all had to be a little brusquer and risk disagreeing with each other so that we could get through the problems faster... without having to mince words... What I was proposing was that it was more than okay to be a bit more confrontational around issues... in order to get everyone's ideas on the table."

Burns learned a number of different communication lessons, sometimes the hard way, during her storied career. While working on her master's degree, in 1980, she began work at Xerox as an intern. Her career officially began the next year when she joined the company full time. She worked in a variety of roles over 36 years, including product development and planning, and as an executive assistant, starting in 1991, to then chairman and CEO, Paul Allaire. She later held high-level positions in global manufacturing, corporate strategic services, and business group operations. She excelled in everything she did. She became president of Xerox in 2007 and, two years later, ascended to the role of chief executive officer. A highlight of her time as CEO was the acquisition of Affiliated Computer Services. She enjoyed all of it. "Xerox turned out to be a wonderful company and perfect for me, though I didn't know that at first... The culture was blue collar with very little hierarchy. People at the highest level carried their own bags, drove their own cars, ate often in the company cafeteria, and mostly flew Coach. The company culture was very people oriented. Problem solving involved discussion, debate, and consensus all the way down to my entry-level work in various engineering labs. Many of the employees had been there for years and years. There was a sense of family and loyalty at Xerox, which had a far lower rate of turnover than other companies." When she took over the top job, Burns obviously endeavored to preserve all that she loved best about the culture, particularly around the importance of good communication.

Two key skills that Burns learned to cultivate over the years were, first, to temper her bluntness and take time to listen to what others had to say - even if she disagreed - and, second, to be honest when delivering feedback to others, but also to seek and accept feedback for herself as well. Wayland Hicks, while he was the number two executive at Xerox, mentored Burns: "Wayland, who remains a dear friend, gave me specific leadership advice. He urged me to hone my bluntness by advising me not to intimidate people and to listen carefully to their ideas instead of dismissing or overruling them. He also cautioned me about my impatience with people who I thought were not good at what they did or didn't carry their weight." Burns readily acknowledges, "I was not always very good at what I did – but I wanted people to tell me when I wasn't. I thrived on input. I was always curious about how people thought I was doing, and not about whether they liked me (even though that would be helpful). I didn't always love the feedback, but I would be more nervous if I didn't get any feedback." There is a very strong argument to be made that listening is the most important communication skill, and the sad fact is that not many of us are very good at it. We are also generally loath to hear feedback, particularly negative (or 'constructive,' depending on your point of view) feedback, but we never get better unless we learn to buck up and listen to the truth.

As her career progressed, Burns came to appreciate the power of a good story, well-told and with authenticity, as a tool to motivate people. In a 2004 article from *Harvard Business Review*, communications expert Stephen Denning asks a very good question: "Do stories really have a role to play in the business world?" He concludes emphatically that they do: "Believe me, I'm familiar with the skepticism about [stories]. When you talk about 'storytelling' to a group of hard-headed executives, you'd better be prepared for some eye rolling... That's because most executives operate with a particular – and generally justified – mind-set. Analysis is what drives business thinking... Yet this strength is also a weakness. Analysis might excite the mind, but it hardly offers a route to the heart." Facts and figures are important, but facts alone are not necessarily what inspires people to survive and succeed in an environment of disruptive change. "Even the most logical arguments usually don't do much to motivate people, but effective storytelling often does. In fact, in certain situations, nothing else works."

Authenticity – just being our own true self - is critical. In 2008, in another piece from *HBR*, consultant Nick Morgan says, "In today's difficult economy... employees and shareholders are more skeptical than ever. Authenticity - including the ability to communicate authentically with others – has become an important leadership attribute. When leaders have it, they can inspire their followers to make extraordinary efforts on behalf of their organizations."

As she became more senior at Xerox, the company provided Ursula Burns with a speech coach. Her coach emphasized to Burns the importance of simply being herself when she presented, but that there were also things she could improve upon. Burns says, "She was very good, unlike a few I'd worked with previously who tried to get me to speak differently, which caused me to lose interest and back away. This speech coach was different. 'How you sound is basically who you are... There's nothing we can do about that – it's just the way it is – so let's look at your content.'" Her coach taught Burns to slow down and enunciate clearly. And she encouraged her to tell stories in the way that worked best for her: "She taught me that whatever story I had to tell had to include the facts, but from my point of view. That was critical for me. She understood that I took comfort in facts and that, for me to become a better, more comfortable speaker, I should center my speech around facts."

For audiences at Xerox, Ursula Burns came across as most truly authentic in her storytelling when she told everyone in plain terms how she felt personally about the facts before them. She gave them an authentic dose of reality, but she also strove to give them hope. "How many times have I heard colleagues using 'corporate-speak,' like when a corporate person responds to a question with big, meaningless phrases out of a business school manual? I couldn't do that. I learned to put my cards on the table from the get-go."

Burns also came to understand the criticality of something that we have all been sorely missing during the time of the pandemic, which is the need for frequent in-person, face-to-face communication. "Employee meetings were a continuous and vital activity. Small meetings, including one-on-one meetings, and very large communication sessions were a normal part of my monthly calendar, and I realized there was no substitution for face-to-face dialogue. I sent out many formal written communications as well as informal notes, but meeting personally with individuals was best for me." The advantages of such a personalized mode of interaction were obvious: "Back-and-forth, open and direct communication yields the best connection and imparts and gathers the best information. It also gave the employees and me a real human connection to one another and minimized misunderstandings."

One of the most important leadership principles is the necessity that leaders establish a common purpose for their team, and to do this effectively requires first-rate communication skills. Burns developed an annual ritual for establishing company direction with her top leaders. She describes the process: "At the start of every year, my leadership team and I held a kickoff event for the top two hundred to three hundred people in the company. We communicated how the company was doing as a whole – what was successful, what needed work – and recognized various types of success, including financial, social engagement, quality, leadership, and innovation. We also laid out the corporate strategy and plans for the year. This was a serious event that was action filled."

In the end, Burns came to realize that the very best leaders developed a keen ability to communicate two things that were of preeminent importance: reality and hope. She concludes: "I practiced what I preached throughout my tenure as CEO. The role of a leader, I'd picked up some years ago from my friend and mentor Ken Chennault [former chairman and CEO of American Express], is to define reality and give hope. Those words were my mantra." The leader who can honestly and accurately communicate to the team their current reality, but then also inspire them with a path forward and hope for the future – as Ursula Burns proves - will indeed be successful in her leadership journey.

*Alone, we can do so little; together,
we can do so much.*

HELEN KELLER

CONCLUSION

In Chapter One, I argued that the first and perhaps most important leadership lesson of the Apollo missions is to demonstrate the power of what can be attained by a diverse team of talented people, dedicated to a common purpose, working together hand-in-hand. I would also submit that the most difficult leadership skill to master is the ability to "influence without authority." A U.S. president, a Fortune 500 CEO, and the boss of Mission Control at NASA have every right to expect that when they give work direction, people on their team will immediately move to action. These powerful people give an order, and things get done (usually, but not always).

Getting things done is not so easy for the individual contributor who has no management authority, and sits in the middle or even closer to the bottom of the organizational hierarchy. If this person needs to get something done, she will need to convince others - those below her, her peer colleagues, or even her boss - to do what she wants. This is a challenging task, not often easily accomplished. Yet it is astounding how many people who are a critical part of the Apollo story were just such individual contributors, striving to do their job every day, to create a positive outcome, and to help achieve the overall objective. These folks are truly unsung heroes.

Katherine Johnson influenced without authority by asking questions. From her obituary in *The Economist*: "In 1953 [when she had just joined the all-male Flight Research Division as a mathematician] women did not question men. They stayed in their place." Most especially, a Black woman stayed in her place. Nevertheless, she began to ask questions, in a direct but careful way. And they were good questions. "She asked more... questions, and they got her noticed." The men came to appreciate that "her incessant 'Why' and 'How' made their work sharper. It also challenged them." In a remarkable career for which she was not fully recognized until near the end of her life, Katherine Johnson learned to plot the trajectories of spacecraft so they could safely leave and then reenter Earth's atmosphere. Alan Shepard's Mercury capsule splashed down safely and right on target in 1961, thanks to Katherine Johnson. John Glenn refused to go into orbit in 1962 without the benefit of her computations confirming his flight path. She calculated timing for the Moon landing of Apollo 11. She devised an improved method for navigating through observation of the stars. Later in her career, she worked on the Space Shuttle. Her contributions were mostly unrecognized at the time, but her impact was enormous.

John Houbolt influenced without authority by never giving up. He was an unknown NASA engineer laboring on problems related to rendezvous and orbital design. He became obsessed with the challenge of creating the most efficient, cost-effective and speedy method for achieving a lunar landing. He studied the idea - building upon the research of others from as far back as the 1920s - of modular spacecraft that would jettison unneeded weight at various points during the mission. Houbolt ran detailed numbers to prove that multiple stages and a separate, dedicated lunar lander would work; this option came to be called Lunar Orbit Rendezvous, or LOR. His colleagues mostly dismissed his work, arguing that what he proposed was far too complicated and risky. Yet Houbolt persisted. He bent the ear of anyone who would listen and, in particular, he had no hesitation in going above the heads of his bosses, all the way up the chain of command to leaders such as Robert Seamans, NASA's new associate administrator. People became exasperated with Houbolt; he, in turn, became so frustrated that at one point he asked: "Do we want to get to the Moon or not?" Through a long and arduous review process, Houbolt stuck to his guns, finally convincing Werner von Braun that his LOR idea represented the best chance of getting a man to the Moon and safely home again. With von Braun's support, Houbolt won the day.

Frances "Poppy" Northcutt influenced without authority by being a trailblazer and overcoming gender discrimination. She was also incredibly smart and damn good at her job. She was an engineer and the first woman at NASA to work in an operational support role at Mission Control, starting in the mid-1960s. Northcutt was interviewed by *Time* magazine in July 2019, and she recalled, "I started as a 'computress,' number crunching. What a weird title. Not only do they think I'm a computer, but they think I'm a gendered computer... During the Apollo 11 mission, I worked on trans-Earth injection – return-to-Earth maneuvers." When asked if she was treated differently based on gender, she said, "During Apollo 8, people would be watching me. I would hear chatter about looking at what's on channel whatever [on our internal camera system]. Finally, at one point, I turned on that channel, and there was a camera just on me... I just went 'O.K., now I know.' There was a lot of sexism [at work]..." Nevertheless, she persevered, and in a demonstration of her enormous talent and status as a true Renaissance Woman, she later worked as a stockbroker, earned a law degree, and currently serves as president of the National Organization for Women in Texas. She felt strongly compelled to join the women's movement, saying, "I became more conscious partly because of the attention I was getting as the first and only woman in my role in the Mission Control Center. It increased my awareness of how limited women's opportunities were. It was almost 1970, we're at the brink of going to the Moon, and we still don't have more women? I should have been 100th."

While there is still a long, long way to go, there is hope that things will continue to improve. In 1961, 13 young women became part of the Women in Space Program. They went through the same rigorous tests as the Mercury astronauts, just to see how they would match up; in the end, across the board, they did as well or better than their male counterparts. Yet, until just recently, none of these tough, talented women would ever fly in outer space.

Of the original group, who were sometimes referred to as the Mercury 13, the best of the best was 21-year-old Wally Funk. She had soloed and earned her pilot's license by age 17. She flew whenever she could, and over the course of her long lifetime (she is now 82) she has logged close to 20,000 flying hours, and been a flight instructor to more than 3,000 fledgling pilots. As the Cold War heated up, NASA cancelled the Women in Space Program. Wally Funk refused to be discouraged. In an interview from the *New York Times* in July 2021, she said, "I was young and I was happy. I just believed it would come. If not today, then in a couple of months." She continued over the years to apply with NASA to be an astronaut, but was repeatedly turned away, purportedly based on her lack of an engineering degree (John Glenn was also without a degree in engineering.)

Years later, when private space travel – through the auspices and thanks to the fortunes of a group of ambitious billionaires such as Elon Musk, Richard Branson and Jeff Bezos - became possible, Wally Funk saw her opportunity. When Bezos invited her to join him and two other men on his Blue Origin rocket for a four-minute trip to outer space in the summer of 2021, she jumped at the chance. The flight was a success, and Wally Funk became the oldest person ever to fly in outer space. She was an inspiration to many. Tanya Harrison, a planetary scientist, said, "Seeing her finally get to go into space decades after proving that she was not only capable, but perhaps more capable than the men she was essentially up against during the Mercury program is so incredible. Her enthusiasm and attitude are positively infectious, and so I hope her flight into space gives her a renewed platform to inspire a whole generation of girls to pursue space or aviation."

Nevertheless, some people have more complicated feelings about Ms. Funk's ride in space. From the *NYT*: "...for many women and nonbinary people involved in space and astronomy, the moment is more nuanced than just a lifelong dream realized. 'On the one hand, I am thrilled for her that she is getting to live this dream she has held for so long,' said Lucianne Walkowicz, an astronomer at the Adler Planetarium in Chicago. 'On the other hand, her individually being granted this opportunity does nothing to address any of the reasons she was previously excluded from going to space, and in fact still poses a man of great privilege – this time specifically Jeff Bezos – as the gatekeeper for her access to space, access which she already earned and deserves." The overarching question becomes: Who is space really for?

● ❭ ❭ ❭ ○ ❲ ❲ ❲ ●

While the Soviet Union put a woman, Valentina Tereshkova, into space in 1963, it was not until 20 years later that an American woman, Dr. Sally Ride, went into orbit. Guion Bluford became the first Black American in space in 1983, and nine years later Mae Jemison became the first Black woman in orbit. Unfortunately, throughout NASA's history, only 18 astronauts have been Black. Currently, out of 48 active-duty NASA astronauts, 16 are women. In recent times, though the numbers are still not where they need to be, women and people of color have become a more important part of the continuing effort to explore space.

In October 2019, astronauts Christina Koch and Dr. Jessica Meir successfully executed the first all-female spacewalk, outside of the International Space Station (ISS). When Koch returned to Earth in February 2021, she had established a record for the longest stay in space by a woman, 328 days (Scott Kelly spent 342 days in space; the all-time American record holder is Peggy Whitson who, over the course of three missions, stayed in space for 665 days.) While aboard the ISS, Koch conducted important research, among many other experiments, around the role of gravity and space on health, cellular development and tissue growth in plants, as well as the impact of growing food in space on human social dynamics – the ability to grow and share healthy food while underway in space will no doubt be critical to future long-duration missions to the Moon or Mars. An analysis in the *NYT* from February 2021 predicts: "In the future, someone will pass [Christina Koch's] endurance records. The first woman will walk on the Moon, NASA promises. Two or more women will go on the first all-woman launch. Perhaps we'll see the first all-woman crew on the ISS. But for now, those missions remain mere potentialities. Ms. Koch has earned her place in the history books, and by crossing these thresholds, has opened the door to the future."

The first woman to set foot on the Moon could very well be Jessica Watkins. In addition to continued and extensive work on the ISS, NASA is increasingly focused on a new program called Artemis, with the objective of sending humans back to the lunar surface by the mid-2020s. In April 2022, Dr. Watkins will become the first Black woman to join the crew of humanity's longest home in orbit, the ISS. She is a planetary geologist from Colorado who will serve as a mission specialist on SpaceX's April flight, called Crew-4, which will shuttle four astronauts to the space station. Once on board, she will spend six months in outer space.

Great leaders work hard at establishing common purpose, developing strong relationships and trust, communicating clearly, continuing to learn, demonstrating energy and passion, and making good decisions. We would never have reached the Moon in the first place without many leaders who possessed these abilities. Great leaders also understand the importance of teamwork and diversity. And great leaders can come from any level within an organization.

In a March 2021 interview in *Scientific American*, Jessica Watkins was asked why diversity will be critical for reaching the ultimate goal – putting human beings back on the Moon - of the Artemis program. She replied, "It's important that the Artemis team be diverse, first of all, because a diverse team is a strong team. The astronaut corps (as well as all of NASA) is made up of people with diverse skill sets, strengths, backgrounds and experiences – and relying on each of those individuals' expertise will enable the collective success of the Artemis missions. The whole is truly greater than the sum of its parts. It's also important because representation does matter. It was absolutely beneficial to me as a young girl to have role models to look up to who looked like me and for them to go before me and create a path for me to pursue my dreams. I hope that the Artemis team can do that for the next generation of explorers and inspire them to follow their dreams as well."

Well said, Dr. Watkins, well said. We all look forward to the glorious day we see you walk upon the surface of the Moon.

ACKNOWLEDGEMENTS

To my friend Dara Beevas, who has published all six of my books, and her excellent team of professionals at Wise Ink Creative Publishing, you are the best. Thanks also to my friend Emily Shaffer Rodvold of Lift-Creative, who has designed all six books, my website, various PowerPoint presentations, logos, my business cards, etc. – you are a really talented, all-purpose superstar, who has helped keep me in business over all these years. To my dear wife Faith and my wonderful daughters Anna and Lucia, thank you for your support and encouragement. I will love you always.

PHOTO CREDITS

Back cover photos, starting top left and moving clockwise (all photos are in the public domain): a Saturn V rocket launches; footprints on the lunar surface; Katherine Johnson, at the age of 97, receives the Presidential Medal of Freedom and a congratulatory kiss from President Barack Obama, November 24, 2015; jubilation in Mission Control with the success of Apollo 11 – President Kennedy's dream realized; a Saturn V in flight; a lunar module on the surface of the Moon; Frances "Poppy" Northcutt began her career at NASA working in computers and then as an engineer for the Apollo program – she became the first female engineer in Mission Control during the Apollo 8 mission.